T0148742

Managing American Hegemony

Managing American Hegemony

★ ★ ★ ★ ★ ★ ★ ★ ★ ★

Essays on Power in a Time of Dominance

★ ★ ★ ★ ★ ★ ★ ★ ★ ★

KORI N. SCHAKE

HOOVER INSTITUTION PRESS

| Stanford University | Stanford, California |

The Hoover Institution on War, Revolution and Peace, founded at Stanford University in 1919 by Herbert Hoover, who went on to become the thirty-first president of the United States, is an interdisciplinary research center for advanced study on domestic and international affairs. The views expressed in its publications are entirely those of the authors and do not necessarily reflect the views of the staff, officers, or Board of Overseers of the Hoover Institution.

www.hoover.org

Hoover Institution Press Publication No. 563

Hoover Institution at Leland Stanford Junior University,
Stanford, California, 94305-6010

Copyright © 2009 by the Board of Trustees of the
    Leland Stanford Junior University
All rights reserved. No part of this publication may be reproduced, stored in a retrieval system, or transmitted in any form or by any means, electronic, mechanical, photocopying, recording, or otherwise, without written permission of the publisher and copyright holders.

First printing 2009
15 14 13 12 11 10 09   9 8 7 6 5 4 3 2 1

Manufactured in the United States of America

♾ The paper used in this publication meets the minimum requirements of the American National Standard for Information Sciences—Permanence of Paper for Printed Library Materials, ANSI / NISO Z39.48-1992.

Library of Congress Cataloging-in-Publication Data
Schake, Kori N.
Managing American hegemony : essays on power in a time of dominance /
Kori N. Schake.
        p.   cm. — (Hoover Institution Press publication series ; 563)
Includes bibliographical references and index.
ISBN 978-0-8179-4901-3 (hardback : alk. paper)
ISBN 978-0-8179-4902-0 (pbk. : alk. paper)
    1. United States—Foreign relations—2001– . 2. Hegemony—United States. I. Title.
JZ1480.S33 2009
327.73—dc22   2008007267

Contents

★ ★ ★

Foreword

★   ★   ★

The Hoover Institution exists, in the words of Herbert Hoover, to "point the road to PEACE, to PERSONAL FREEDOM, and to the SAFEGUARDS OF THE AMERICAN SYSTEM." This mission is advanced through the dissemination of ideas that encourage positive policy formation using reasoned arguments and intellectual rigor, converting conceptual insights into practical initiatives judged to be beneficial to society.

Managing American Hegemony, by Hoover research fellow Kori Schake, is just such an undertaking. In it she articulates the elements of power, broadly defined, that form the safeguards of the American way of life.

The success of the United States in the international order cannot be taken for granted. Indeed, the freedom and prosperity our generation enjoys is not guaranteed for our children and grandchildren. Only by understanding the forces that have resulted in American power can we hope to preserve the moral, military, and financial strength that ensures our liberty.

Schake's precise contribution identifies the convergence of elements—economic, military, diplomatic, linguistic, and cultural—that reinforce American hegemony. The roots of our success stem from a dynamic political culture, where change is championed, individuals are rewarded for risk, and the structures of society adapt and grow with the nation. Schake offers an insightful look at the current state of U.S. power and how we can address fiscal, political, and organizational threats to our continued prosperity.

It is fitting that such a book would be written by Kori. Her experience as a scholar, teacher, and principal within various government agencies, makes her uniquely qualified for the task. She served as a senior policy advisor to the presidential campaign of John McCain; prior to that she was Principal Deputy Director in the Secretary of State's Office of Policy Planning—both roles demonstrate the broad knowledge and wide-ranging thinking necessary to undertake such a book.

A review of her experience includes the Bradley Professor of International Security Studies at the United States Military Academy at West Point and director for Defense Strategy and Requirements on the National Security Council during President George W. Bush's first term. Her political, military, and security research has been recognized and supported by a MacArthur Foundation Research and Writing Award and numerous academic fellowships.

We want to thank Barbara and Tom Stephenson for their significant ongoing support of the Hoover Institution and the work of Kori Schake. Tom, currently serving as U.S. Ambassador to Portugal, is that rare individual who contributes both intellectually and financially to the Hoover Institution.

There can be no more critical field of public policy than the study of economic, political, and societal relationships that shape the international order and profoundly impact foreign policy, security, and trade. With *Managing American Hegemony,* Kori Schake grounds our understanding of the world in the reality of U.S. predominance. In doing so, she helps shed light on the reality of order, stability, and peace that America's presence brings. Her words are valued now more than ever in an age of American skepticism.

JOHN RAISIAN
Tad and Diane Taube Director
Hoover Institution
Stanford University

Acknowledgments

⋆ ⋆ ⋆

This is not a book of scholarship: too much is asserted rather than proven, data provided is illustrative but frequently not systematic. It is, however, a book of ideas, intended to inform public policy debates about our country and the changing international order. It was written in the interlude between my work on the National Security Council and joining the State Department's Policy Planning Staff, to address questions my work there had raised and that I believed were in many cases not explained accessibly enough in the existing literature about how globalization is changing the international order and what it means for the United States. While the arguments advanced would certainly be strengthened by additional research, broader peer review, and revisions, I hope the ideas will nonetheless be of interest to scholars, national security practitioners, and people like my wonderful Mother, who does not work in this field but reads widely and cares about these issues.

I am profoundly grateful to the Hoover Institution for supporting this work. John Raisian's commitment to engaging academics in the country's crucial public policy debates has been a constant source of inspiration. Tod Lindberg, the cheerful and serious-minded Vicar of Hoover's Washington office, nourished this effort and me in innumerable ways. Peter Berkowitz gave me the opportunity to present some of this work to several informed and critical audiences (including his sharp self). Under the terrific stewardship of Colonel Mike Meese, the Department of Social Sciences at the U.S. Military Academy let me use my post as Distinguished Chair in International Security Studies to test-drive these ideas on some of the country's sparkliest and most committed young people. More than anyone else, Major Jon Byrom, my Executive Officer in the Department of Social Sciences at West Point, helped me think these issues through as we taught together. He undertook the research presented in the table, challenged my ideas where they didn't accord with his research or experience—even bet me money on the proof of several questions we were thinking our way through. My thanks to them all.

Introduction

★   ★   ★

This is a book about American power: why it's so predominant in the international order, whether it's likely to remain so, and how current practices can be revised to reduce the cost to the United States of managing the system. Despite clarion calls about the end of the unipolar moment and the demise of American moral and military and financial power, the United States remains the defining state in the international system and is likely to be so for at least several more decades. If there were a market for state power, now would be a great time to buy futures in American power. The commodity is substantially undervalued, and the market does not yet seem to have noticed.

Why is that? Partly because the short-term indicators look dicey. The dollar has lost 40 percent of its value in eighteen months and appears set to fall further as the dimensions of the subprime mortgage crisis become clearer. Government debt is $30 thousand per person and growing at the rate of a half-trillion dollars a year in deficit spending. American choices about responding to terrorism are shocking to many of our friends, who question our deservingness to set international norms and their interest in maintaining a close association with U.S. policies and values. The American military seems incapable of producing victories in either Afghanistan or Iraq, fostering questions about whether military force continues to be a salient characteristic of state power and whether American strategy is too militaristic to succeed against current challenges. The American government is alarmingly incapable of orchestrating the elements of its own power.

The cacophonous American debate about all these issues further concerns non-Americans, as does a political system that throws up amateurs into the highest offices of the world's most powerful nation. Europeans even joke about how they should get to vote in American elections because their well-being is so influenced by American policies, but Americans take no account of that in choosing our political leaders. And yet, the stubbornly local focus and cultural predilections of American citizens are the great strength of the country. International observers since de Tocqueville have marveled at the vibrancy of American civil society. We are a people made great by distrust of our own government; as a result, responsibility centers on the individual and encourages civic activism in other venues, such as religion and philanthropy. These turn out to be enormous advantages as globalization makes possible the ever greater empowerment of individuals. What it takes to be successful domestically in America is also what it takes to be successful internationally in a globalizing order.

American society has adapted to globalization remarkably well. The resilience with which Americans have found new professions as manufacturing migrated to cheaper labor markets contrasts favorably with the revanchist efforts by other wealthy states to artificially (and expensively) preserve the eroding status quo rather than encourage and shape change. It helps that the American economy is an engine of job creation, but that is a result of explicit choices about labor market flexibility. The signature advantage of the American economy is the risk tolerance of its work force: the economy sheds jobs and creates jobs, and people mostly accept that the nature of economic activity is uncertain. It is a simple but remarkable attribute, especially in a country with so little government effort to cushion labor transition.

The adaptability of American workers mirrors the general malleability of the country. The "invitation to struggle" that the Constitution enshrines in American institutions of governance fosters a constant debate on social issues that is messy (and often inadvertently hilarious) to watch but serves to keep pressing issues under evaluation as persuasion and litigation shape our domestic space. The constant negotiation over who we are makes us amenable to redefinition, and that allows American culture to cherry-pick elements of other cultures to improve our own. In a globalizing order in which many societies are attempting to shield their traditions from external influence, American culture voraciously seeks out and incorporates new elements that further broaden its appeal.

The risk tolerance of American society makes us less averse to the growing uncertainty and permeability of societies that globalization is creating. Americans are so accepting of change and risk that we have come to exemplify what others fear—globalization is often equated with Americanization. The tumult of rapid capital flows, labor priced out of its own domestic market, and overwhelming cascades of information that we have already largely adapted to domestically are being unleashed on societies everywhere with stampeding force, and states are struggling to keep pace. Governments have numerous incentives to blame the marauding forces of global capitalism and American influence rather than take responsibility for poorly managing the changing rules of the international order.

American success is, not surprisingly, resented by states and societies that have not found ways to preserve what they value. Societies with "better" but less popular attributes feel affronted that the accessibility of American society and culture has such broad appeal. The equation that makes the United States so successful is not difficult to discern, but difficult to put into practice, especially if societies clamor for the economic enrichment, innovation, and durable social peace of American society without wanting to endure its fractiousness, economic insecurity, and permeability. For these reasons, despite the near-term shortcomings, American power is likely to dominate the international order for at least another half century.

The genius of the American-dominated international order is in establishing and enforcing rules that not only benefit American interests but provide others with paths to enrichment and influence. We have built an international order that permits the peaceful rise of dynamic countries. Their success challenges America to greater innovation and activity, which keeps our economy agile and our influence expanding. It is a virtuous cycle: the more countries that opt into the order, the more beneficial for both them and us. As long as America continues to be the most adaptive of societies, we are likely to continue to grow stronger as others also do. It might not look much like a collusive international order amid the rancor of international reaction to Bush administration policies, but that is the trend, and it is reinforced by the apparent lack of alternative: states do not grow rich or powerful outside the American order, and as a result, nearly all opt in.

Perhaps other states could find new paths to power: forming authoritarian societies with market economies, exploiting minorities to strengthen the majority, discovering essential resources, banding together by several states to damage American interests. These things are all possible, but they don't appear likely. The international order is therefore probably stuck with American hegemony, unless we destroy it ourselves.

Several choices of the past decade have caused some to question whether the United States isn't well along the way to that self-inflicted devastation already. Many traditional American allies are repositioning themselves to be more independent. Countries that might have seemed natural allies of the United States are uninterested in association. The dollar is losing its status as the reserve currency of the global financial system. Wall Street is no longer the capital market of choice for firms listing shares. New problems have emerged that other states are reluctant to help manage on the terms the United States has set. An order that has been relatively inexpensive to maintain feels to Americans to be growing costlier, and with fewer states willing to share the burden. The United States is at odds with nearly every international institution, and those the United States is not bickering with (like the International Monetary Fund) seem to avoid the disputatiousness only through their declining relevance.

This prima facie evidence is misleading, however. While the Bush administration's refrain is dangerously self-serving when it asserts that only history can judge its efforts in a time of such momentus change, the truth is that the international order is midstream in a realignment of historic proportions because of globalization and the ways states deal with those changes. The "post–cold war order" is becoming a historical period identifiable by its central characteristics: rapid change; economic insecurity; free movement of people, capital, and goods; emergence of unanticipated threats; states and institutions stressed in new ways to harness change to positive effect rather than be its victims. These are, however, circumstances that already characterize American society to a greater degree than they do most others. We are predisposed by domestic circumstance to manage this international change well.

Our strategic challenge will be persuading others to share the burdens of maintaining the existing order that has served us all so well. To sustain its role as rule setter of the international order, the United States will need to enforce the order in ways others find more comfortable. The costs of the existing order are relatively low because nearly all of the states in the international order voluntarily acquiesce to American predominance. When they stop believing, as some already have, that American power is a force for the general good, the cost of maintaining order increases. It is not enough for us to appreciate that we are a beneficent hegemon; we must do better to demonstrate it to others who are not convinced.

Moreover, the problems threatening America as hegemon—especially terrorism—are not principal concerns for most states in the international order. Compared with managing the ravages of HIV-AIDS on the labor force, managing the food scarcity caused by environmental change, or establishing basic governance and education, America's preoccupation with terrorism appears a luxury many states would prefer to their own problems. It is therefore in our interest to devote more attention to solving the problems we are not afflicted with but that are essential to securing the assistance of the states in which the problems are growing, and so burnish the congeniality of American power.

America is unlikely to drive down the cost of sustaining the international order through an intellectually elegant Grand Strategy, through "strategic communications," or through major government initiatives. These are the equivalent of swinging for the center field fence, looking for the one fat pitch you can connect with that will clear the bases and remove the necessity of taking advantage of every small opportunity and marginal advantage you have in the game. The grand strategic approach is ill-suited to the nature of the challenges in a globalizing order, which are increasing the vulnerability of systems to individual or small-scale action. It is also ill-suited to the nature of American society, because a government organized with so many checks and balances is unlikely to produce ringing clarity of purpose and centrally directed activity.

Instead of struggling against our own national character to produce a grand strategy and unitary effort to govern the international order effectively, we should embrace the very things that have made us successful in the first place: a civil society that undertakes independent activity, the government incentives for private endeavor, and the diversity of effort that provides a laboratory for policy innovation. As a government, we need to stop trying to control activity and instead encourage more modest initiatives to advance our general objectives. This is what any baseball fan would recognize as a small-ball strategy: dominate the game through knowing the strengths and weaknesses in the rosters, judging when to run risks, and making use of every chance to scrape a little scoring together.

In thinking about American power, the first-order question is relevance: who cares? Does it really matter whether America is an empire or a colossus or merely the strongest power in the order? If we are profligate with our power, would it make any difference? State power crescendos and ebbs, empires crumble; this is the nature of the international system. The individual and societal choices would seem largely irrelevant when arrayed against the big arrows of history. And yet the height of the oscillation does matter, and the frequency does, as well. It matters to the states that rely on our strength for their existence or freedom of action. It will matter enormously to Americans if we lose that freedom for ourselves. For no hegemony will last forever, and the way we behave as the strongest power in the order—the norms and rules and precedents we set and enforce—will someday affect how we are constrained when we lack the latitude to act with impunity. The good management of American hegemony will therefore affect the height of our rise, its duration, and even the options available to us in decline.

Understanding why we have succeeded is essential to making sound choices about what to sustain and how to approach the task. This book is organized around six questions:

1. Why is there such concern about American power, especially from the friends and allies of the United States?
2. What accounts for America's stunning success in the round of globalization that swept across the international order at the end of the twentieth century?
3. Are American advantages enduring or transitory?
4. Is the American military still dominant, and does it matter?
5. Can our alliances and international institutions be revised to better align with an extended period of hegemony?
6. On what issues should the next president focus to build an even stronger foundation of American power?

The Fear of Americanization

Chapter 1 explores various explanations for international concern about American dominance in the international order. While there have always been anti-Americanism and arguments about moral equivalency between the United States and its adversaries, the intensity has been magnified with the spread of globalization. Questions about the legitimacy of American power and about our penchant for acting unilaterally predate the Bush administration but have been sharpened by the disregard it has evinced for melding together American interests with those of the international order. The main policy lines of international issues, however, have not varied widely from late Clinton administration choices—a fact many American critics are willfully ignoring in the hope a new presidential administration will magically return to the mythical world of a comfortably multilateral United States taking responsibility for solving everyone's problems. But America is different after September 11, lonelier and more cognizant of its power and uniqueness, which may cause it to allow greater upheaval in the international order in coming years.

Some elements of our uniqueness rankle other states and societies because they feel the juggernaut of our economic, military, and cultural power to a greater degree than Americans, even after September 11, appreciate. Our economy constitutes 25 percent of the entirety of global economic activity and drives the economies of all other major economies. Our military is without peer operationally, fueled by a defense budget larger than that of the next sixteen spenders combined. Our language is the accepted norm, our currency the reserve holding of choice, our entertainment industry the global trendsetter, our citizenship the port of first resort. What makes American dominance so overwhelming is the collusion of so many different facets of power: hard military power, soft cultural power, short-term influence, long-term rule setting. We exemplify the changes many states and societies fear—they are afraid of the disruption globalization is bringing and lack confidence in their ability to shield themselves from its effects.

Because of the magnitude of American power, it is surprising there have been so few successful attempts to overtly curtail it. European allies were able to make the International Criminal Court (ICC) applicable to nonsignatories, but even its most ardent advocates don't imagine attempting to enforce it against Americans. The Chirac government's attempt in 2003 to lead an international movement opposing the U.S. invasion of Iraq had notably few takers. The Shanghai Cooperation Organization may one day prove troublesome, but Russia's behavior toward other members is likelier to result in their seeking the U.S. interest. Likewise Venezuelan President Hugo Chavez's "Bolivarian revolution," which despite oil money to slosh around has few adherents.

The Metrics of Power

Chapter 2 attempts to take the measure of American power in the international order. Experts speak of American power as surpassing that of the Roman Empire at its height, but few imaginative metrics have been used to give a feel for how different and strong the United States is. Most experts settle for gross domestic product (GDP) and defense spending as a proportion of world total—which, at 25 percent and 50 percent, are indeed impressive. However, they fail to give the texture of American power.

Americans have structural advantages in the global competition: language; early availability of the Internet; government, corporate, and university participation in, and support for, technological development. What appears unique about the American dominance of this round of globalization is the degree to which our national mythology of opportunity and individual achievement is being reinforced by the empowerment of individuals through globalization: the difficulties other states and societies experience in the loosening control over elements of their societies are likely to keep America dominant in the international order.

Globalization, simply defined, is the ability of individuals and groups to leap over local barriers into greater opportunity, whether they are seeking information, market access, political mobilization, or investments. We are seeing the modern equivalent of Portuguese explorers and Dutch and British merchants expanding markets and allowing them to operate more efficiently. This expansion is often considered to occur at the expense of state control, which is not strictly true: states retain the ability to regulate activity that occurs within their territory and markets. But states are slower to master the rules of this dizzyingly fast, complex new connectedness, and many make self-serving explanations for their failures in adapting.

Globalization portends a competition among states for talent, as Richard Rosecrance has argued.[1] By extension, the soundest policies for governments facing the onslaught of globalization are investing in human capital and becoming magnets for individuals disaffected from other societies. While the United States underinvests in development (education, transition assistance, etc.), the fundamentals of our political culture appear to substitute. Most potent are the risk tolerance (a societal belief that failure is inherently linked to success and should therefore be lightly stigmatized, settling responsibility on the individual for his or her success or failure), transparency of government as the bulwark against abuse, diversity of our own population making the perquisites of domestic success comparable to the terms of international success, a cultural ethos that attracts many of the most talented and hardworking immigrants, and the advantages of being the international rule setter and guarantor (for they are inextricably linked).

The United States is so predominant because its economic power is undergirded by inventiveness and productivity, its society replenishing and redefining itself through immigration, its language the cultural and business standard, its popular culture the most accessible and enjoyable to diverse groups. Globalization requires a mainframe or standard for integration. For a host of reasons and without a grand governmental plan for hegemony, America's language, culture, and economic practices have become the architecture of globalization.

Sustainability

That America has been successful is, of course, no guarantee of future success. Chapter 3 examines potential challenges to American hegemony. Because of U.S. dependencies on the immigration of talent and on the accessibility of raw materials, and less expensive manufactur-

---

1. Richard Rosecrance, "The Rise of the Virtual State: Territory Becomes Passe," *Foreign Affairs* (July/August 1996).

ing bases, and because of the importance of financial and other service sectors to American prosperity, should globalization falter, American power would falter along with it. A backlash against globalization or the American "brand," the legislation by governments of restraints, voluntary boycotts mobilized by activists, or the loss of interest in or access to opportunities for students and immigrants in the United States would all be damaging but fortunately also appear unlikely.

States have undersold their ability to influence the way globalization affects their societies. Whether for short-term capital investment, long-term structural investment, shipment of goods and services, immigration or emigration of people, states still set the legal frameworks that make mutability of their borders possible. The contrast between the 1998 Asian currency crisis and the 2001 terrorist attacks on the United States demonstrates the difference made by smart government choices in bad circumstances. Asian governments could have enacted laws to limit the speed or magnitude of capital outflows, kept large reserves of foreign currencies to sell during a panic to shore up the value of their own currencies, or put their leading bankers and diplomats to work cajoling ameliorative foreign intervention. Unwillingness or incapacity in those areas left economies vulnerable to an impoverishing crisis.

By comparison, the U.S. mitigation of the economic effects of the September 11 terrorist attacks is a case study in good management. To prevent a potentially catastrophic economic shock, political leaders effectively used the means available to them, including the existing regulations for closing down the stock market when losses exceeded known bands of value, and the advantage of having prior government incentives for companies to create redundant operations, allowing many firms to quickly restart operations. Government was quick to let the most respected economic figure (Fed Chairman Alan Greenspan) lead public and private efforts to calm markets. Crucially, the United States benefited from its global connectedness, since governments and businesses around the world had a common interest in preventing precipitous collapse. It is perhaps the best and most underappreciated example of what the United States is capable of when it capitalizes on its advantages.

There are three basic kinds of prospective challenges to U.S. hegemony: (1) failure to prevent or match the rise of a more powerful state or collective of states; (2) domestic corrosion or ossification based on our domestic weaknesses; and (3) the burden of our international obligations diverting needed effort from domestic priorities.

The rise of an unstoppable competitor is a staple of international relations, usually fanned by attributing to the rising power all of our advantages with none of our difficulties; currently, China is playing the role of manipulative ingenue to America's weakening success. But the difficulties China faces are enormous: rising worker expectations, transition from a manufacturing base to an innovative economy, and an opaque political system ill-tuned to accommodating public concern. China may not prove successful when forced to confront the problems American society is already managing reasonably well, and for cultural reasons is unlikely to supplant the United States as a magnet for talent in the great global competition.

The United States also usually has a cultural affinity for rising powers; their behavior is comprehensible to us because it tends to be how we would, and do, behave, and we expend effort to get the relationships aligned effectively. The United States is more likely to be challenged by, and fail to find the basis of common interest with, unsuccessful countries. A prosperous, confident China does not of necessity diminish American power, as the postwar success of Germany and Japan illustrates. The architecture of the international order America designed accommodates rising powers, and their interests have often colluded with America's own. The order is voluntary, and the benefits are often what rising powers want: prosperity, peace, and the United States taking an interest in their problems. The Chinese appear to be opting into the order—preserving advantages where they can but not seeking to overturn the order—because they are confident of their success.

The European Union is also posited as a potential supplanter of American power, because of its combined GDP and strong consensus on political, economic, and values issues. The EU's answers to many questions are more comforting to many states and societies than the sharp edges of American approaches. Despite its substantial achievements, an EU-centric international order is unlikely because of persisting national frictions, questionable accountability by EU institutions to voters, unwillingness to guarantee security, and internal difficulty coming to terms with diversity, a difficulty that will continue to inhibit the migration of talent to the EU zone.

Domestic corrosion is the second means of dethronement for American power, and our many failings give heft to this school of thought. The scale of government and personal indebtedness are scandalous but seem no impediment to further profligacy. Infrastructure essential to the movement of people, goods, and services is crumbling, and government is failing to invest in its replenishment, much less providing the education and incentives needed for a new technological infrastructure that would be economically expansive. The political system seems to grow more polarized and focused on trivialities. And yet venality is not a new development in American democracy; parental and individual initiative manages with surprising frequency to overcome educational limitations, and local or private efforts frequently compensate for federal incapacity. It is at least unproven that the American system that produced this peace and prosperity is incapable of correcting itself. Thanks to the founding fathers' tying accountability tightly in the structure of the political system, it is more likely that the critique will stimulate the correction than be a harbinger of decline.

Imperial overstretch posits that the responsibilities the United States has undertaken will eventually sap its strength. As with central bank intervention in the market to deflate stock or housing bubbles, discerning when the benefits have reached their zenith is nearly impossible. With defense spending at only 3.5 percent of GDP, and an economy that so manifestly benefits from international engagement, the United States is unlikely to be hobbled by foreign entanglements. We tend to be skeptical of international obligation, wanting each case to be justified in its time against the inherent Jacksonian tradition in American political culture.

It can be argued with some justification that the Iraq War is an example of imperial overstretch. However, even with the price of oil doubling since 2003, the American economy has been remarkably able to absorb the costs with little perturbation in employment or contraction of growth. There has not been an onslaught of political or military challenges to American interests. Vulnerable countries have not abjured U.S. assistance for their protection or sought alternative guarantors. The volunteer military is (admittedly with some strain) meeting its recruiting goals and continues to be the most respected institution in American society. Moreover, Americans are likely to set a higher standard of proof for their government—and the branches of government for each other—for future preemptive wars than they did after the shock of September 11, again showing the self-correcting nature of American power. The way in which Iraq has affected American power is to make its maintenance marginally more costly.

Military Force

The strength of the American military has long been considered a paramount advantage in the international order for the United States and its allies. With the end of the cold war, countries throughout the order took "peace dividends," not only reducing their military capabilities but questioning whether military force would continue to play a defining role in the international order. Using relations among the market democracies as the baseline, most of America's allies have come to believe that soft power—the brand of a society's values—is not only preferable but more effective in shaping state and societal behavior internationally. In most developed countries, members of the military have come to be seen as uniformed social workers: a force to send where suffering is occurring, to give humanitarian assistance and foster economic development.

America remains an outlier among friends in its insistence that killing and destruction are central elements of state power, essential in protecting and advancing the state's interests. Soft power is largely outside a government's control and incapable of being marshaled for a specific purpose on the timeline the government needs to act within. Its effective application requires a level of understanding of foreign countries that the U.S. government (and most other governments) rarely possess. Soft power also has not proven effective in enforcing the rules of the international order—it may help create them, and reduce the cost of upholding them, but cannot enforce them.

The military might to coerce behavior, or to punish states that will not be coerced, is essential to enforcing the rules but often fails to achieve the intended effect, even when its wielder is the hegemon of the international order. The main reason this is so is that governments have complicated political and economic objectives that military force is incapable of achieving. Edmund Burke best characterized the limitations: "The use of force is but temporary. It may subdue for a moment but does not remove the necessity of subduing again; and a country is not to be governed that is perpetually to be conquered."[2] Military force can hold a situation in place while political, economic, cultural, institutional, and other means of shaping societies take place, but it cannot produce those effects.

American leaders tend to use military means more than other states do, partly because this accords with our role as guarantor of the order, but also because we have not invested in the other means of power that would expand our range of tools. America has 1.2 million military servicemembers but only six thousand diplomats and only a handful of staffers working on international issues in the Treasury, Energy, Education, or Agriculture Departments. It is difficult to imagine a genuinely integrated American strategy when departments other than the military lack the numbers to be involved around the world.

Thirty-five years into an all-volunteer force, and with the military composing less than 1 percent of the population, American political leaders often have little familiarity with their own military. This tends toward three errors: too great a deference for the military in spending, too little deference for military judgment in operations, and a propensity to use the military as a venue for changing social norms.

A primer on the American military would require understanding the money and the people. A tabulation of the total cost of American national security includes spending on the military, current operations, homeland defense, and intelligence: it amounts to roughly $695 billion, or $2,317 a year for every person in the country. Even in the narrower confines of budgeted outlays (just the cost of recruiting, training, and equipping the military forces, not employing them), the United States spends five times more than any other country, and of the next top sixteen spenders, only China and Russia are not unequivocally friendly toward the United States. Such an economy of scale produces technologically innovative weapons. But it does not bring the soldiers, sailors, airmen, and marines that are its essence. Opportunity, professional challenges, and public appreciation attract talented people and work to keep them motivated. These things exemplify a culture of which Americans are rightly proud.

Despite all these advantages, the United States has been unable to

2. Edmund Burke, "Second Speech on Conciliation with America" (1775), quoted in Edmund Burke, *Burke's Speech on Conciliation with America,* ed. Hammond Lamont (Boston: Ginn and Co., 1997).

quickly win wars in Iraq and Afghanistan, which should rightly return us to the question of whether military power continues to be the defining tool of international order. This failure should also raise the question of whether the American approach is a cost-effective and sustainable one for the challenges the country is facing.

The United States has not won in Iraq because the task was inherently extremely challenging. The administration made it even more demanding by badly translating the president's political objectives into military objectives and by circumscribing the military's ability to plan and provide resources for the missions; and it was unable to produce the political, social, and economic effects among Iraqis on which success depended. That we have not yet succeeded in Iraq does not by extension mean all wars are unwinnable or that military power is less valuable in shaping the international order.

It does, however, give reason to review the magnitude of defense spending relative to the threats America is facing, especially since the current spending level is very likely unsustainable. Do we really need a military twice as expensive as the one we had in 2000 to protect our interests? The next quadrennial defense review should be conducted with four objectives: answering first-order questions about the nature and magnitude of current threats; developing cost-effective strategies for combating those threats; challenging shibboleths like traditional service budget slices; and creating incentives for innovation. Our failures in Iraq should also precipitate debate about whether American national security objectives would be more effectively attained by increasing spending in nondefense areas rather than by continuing to improve on what we already do well.

Because using force badly—whether by military or, as in Iraq, by governmental incapacity—not only dishonors the sacrifices our military makes but also devalues the currency of military force. For if countries and organizations believe we cannot apply our military power effectively to protect and advance our interests, confidence in us as a guarantor will decline and challenges to our interests will rise—the cost of maintaining the international order will rise substantially for us. America has work to do in rebuilding confidence in our ability to use force effectively.

The consciousness of force as an integral part of state behavior is a rarity among the world's wealthiest and most powerful countries. The United States benefits substantially from being the guarantor of security for friends and countries on which the prosperity of our economy rests; most other countries with the ability to provide security no longer have domestic support for using military force to impose their will.

Alliances and Institutions

Many American allies are eagerly anticipating a change of administration after the 2008 elections, mistakenly believing that after an extended period of unpopularity and difficulties in Iraq, the United States will return chastened, pliable, and multilateral-minded to take the lead in solving common security problems in ways more comfortable to European sensibilities. This is unlikely to occur. The continuity between administrations as terrorism has come to dominate American thinking on security is more pronounced than either the Clinton or Bush administrations would like to acknowledge.

Rancorous electoral debate will also mask the similarity, but it is striking how little candidates' views actually differ on the main policy issues: aggressively fighting terrorism, protecting the American homeland, preempting threats, preferring unilateralism as a widely accepted means of advancing American interests, preponderantly using military force to achieve national goals, developing energy independence to shield ourselves from sinister suppliers, supporting Israel in Palestine, deploying missile defenses despite the objections of allies whose vulnerability may increase, and paying little attention to—much less making expensive or substantive compromise on—issues at the center of allied concern, such as global warming.

American power came to dominate the international order because of its attractiveness, but the way in which the Bush administration has asserted that power has somewhat diminished its magnetism, causing us to pay a higher premium for what we need to do in the world. International institutions generate enormous frustration among Americans because despite our being the majority stakeholder in most of them, and despite all our expenditure of effort, they often are unhelpful. They seem as often as not venues for anti-American grandstanding or for recalcitrant states' withholding support. Participation in international institutions is unquestionably frustrating for the United States: representativeness often diminishes effectiveness; the compromises needed to build international consensus reduce the consistency and bite of policies; we are locked into rules that tax us substantially more than other participants; and states often justify inaction by stymieing institutions.

All true, and yet institutions are valuable for legitimating the power of the strong through the consent of the weak. As America is the strongest state in the international order, it has the greatest potential to benefit, if we can stop struggling against what international institutions do poorly and better match our efforts to their abilities.

It is not, however, in American interests to perpetuate alliances and institutions as they now exist. The United Nations is too powerful as a legitimating body and too irresponsible as an acting body. The North Atlantic Treaty Organization (NATO) requires enormous American effort to produce the modest political and military activity it undertakes. We are overinvested in some relationships that were created for earlier threats, and we have allowed the constraints of those relations to be extrapolated into new circumstances in ways that impede our management of current threats. We are underinvested in relationships that have the potential to pull rising powers into positive-sum activity and to encourage friendly middle powers to take leadership roles. We are too much concerned about activity by institutions we are not members of, and too little concerned about the danger of capable contributors to international peace and security remaining passive. That the United States built these international institutions is not enough reason to sustain them; that they give the United States ways to shift from an unsatisfactory status quo to a more advantageous set of practices and relationships is.

Former Secretary General Kofi Annan was right when he told UN members that the organization needs to make itself more useful or it will become irrelevant to security. NATO is not succeeding at the test of Afghanistan. But in both cases, it is worth considerable U.S. effort to keep its shoulder to the wheel in the work for reform and fairer burden sharing, using the threat of an alternative organization emerging should they not succeed. Europeans are seeking to extrapolate their privileged position in relation to U.S. policy making to new issues where their contribution seldom merits it. Claims by European allies that they are the most capable allies of the United States only serve to highlight how little of their potential they translate into kinetic international action.

The concert of democracies would be a great thing if only democratic states were more willing to contribute to solving problems; we are more likely to find substantial contributors from among the less virtuous but more self-interested states. As such, the United States should gently shift toward rewarding contribution rather than like-mindedness in our international relations. The Bush administration has begun this effort with the Proliferation Security Initiative and attempts to manage global warming issues outside the Kyoto framework. There are so many problems to solve, and discussing what should be but is not being done does not equate to solving them. The United States needs to shift its focus from those we like best to those most inclined to contribute.

Many opportunities exist for greater common activity with China in ways that not only solve practical problems and ease tensions among America's existing Asian allies but also increase the likelihood of China's accepting the U.S.'s hope of China's becoming a "responsible stakeholder." India poses similar opportunities. Establishing close bilateral cooperation and extending it to more participants should be an urgent priority for the United States, so that we create a different and more beneficial dynamic in our international relations.

Bilaterally empowering friendly states to take leadership roles in solving problems should also be a priority for U.S. policy. Australia was persuaded to take the lead in East Timor because of U.S. commitments to underwrite its success. The model enabled the Australian government to become more active as a regional leader, fostered its participation in later operations, and emboldened Australians to take responsibility and solve important problems. By underwriting the success of allies, the United States builds for itself more capable allies and nurtures the awareness in states of their own strength.

Coalitions of the willing may be unpopular among America's "permanent allies" and have detrimental effects on political and military capital in the short to medium term, but unless the established institutions become dramatically more effective at providing political consensus and hard power contributions, they will be supplanted by temporary partnering focused on solving specific problems. The extent of U.S. obligation as the guarantor of security argues strongly for the United States to invest extensively in such relationships to tackle local problems and build goodwill so that countries will take an interest in our concerns.

Where traditional alliances and relationships, such as NATO, continue to make sense, the United States should fold nonallies into the routine and make possible NATO building blocks to larger international coalitions. Expanding the conversation beyond Europe will give America's

European allies a better sense of the other forces shaping U.S. views and actions and expose these allies to regional expectations that they will contribute to solving problems. Using the Supreme Allied Commander Europe (SACEUR) in the U.S. policy process to negotiate specific missions in larger operations could provide Europeans the status they seek and better match their contributions to functional needs. The approach need not replace a jealously guarded bilateral cooperation, just expand the range of choice for NATO allies.

The United States also has many tools to affect allied attitudes, and we could use them to much greater effect by treating international politics more like domestic politics: lobby parliamentarians, suggest stories to journalists, demonstrate the local effects of international action, mobilize interest groups. Our tendency is to work with governments and to centralize representation in capitals, rather than working with civil society to affect governments. Imagine, for example, how much more difficult it would have been for Jacques Chirac to oppose the war in Iraq if the United States had taken the debate to the suburbs of any large French city, arguing that we were trying to create a Middle East from which people would not have to emigrate for political freedom and economic opportunity.

Too often in foreign policy, the United States plays to our weaknesses instead of our strengths. An approach to alliances and institutions that encourages other states to take responsibility for solving problems and leading needed institutional reforms; accepts variance from our preferred outcome as the price of not solving the problem ourselves; affects attitudes in allied countries by participating in their domestic debates; and assists in the resourcing and effort, would serve to lower the risk of an international order in which states are unwilling to step forward and contribute to solutions. Otherwise, we will be expected to solve every problem; states that could contribute will not, and we will be confronted with criticism from states that run no risks and therefore underestimate the difficulty of solving international problems.

Self-Help

America has the enviable advantage that the means of sustaining its power in the international order are largely in American hands. What the next American president chooses to do, or neglects to address, on four important issues will in large measure set the trajectory of American power. The next presidency will be defined by choices about dealing with the national debt, whether we need to fight a war on terror, how to leave Iraq, and improving our ability to carry out comprehensive strategies. Each question carries costs and risks with systemic repercussions. Unless the President addresses these issues as priorities, incremental decisions about budgets and events will set the country's course.

Debt. Reducing our debt is the simplest and most difficult challenge facing the country. It is so glaring a vulnerability and its magnitude so staggering that it beggars useful comparison: the government has incurred debts of $30 thousand for every person in the country, and with disappointingly little to show for the price tag. Continuing such profligacy will eventually erode long-term confidence in the United States as the rule setter of the global order and in the dollar as a prime holding currency. Debt servicing on the loans will absolutely grow more expensive and crowd out other kinds of government spending.

There is no investment the U.S. government could make, or capability it could acquire, that would add as much to American power and to a stable, prosperous international order as would paying down our national debt. Breaking the cycle of deficit spending will grow harder, not easier, as the severity of reduction grows commensurate with the size of the debt. We are now facing no catastrophic challenge that justifies an unbalanced budget or perpetuating this enormous debt. Political leaders are averting their eyes from their responsibility to keep the country on a stable footing economically because trade-offs will be politically unpopular and painful. And yet this window of prosperity and dominance in the international order is the best time to accept near-term sacrifice and risk to ensure long-term well-being. If we cannot do it now, we cannot do it, and we will have sown the seeds of our own demise.

Terrorism. Whether to continue fighting a "war on terror" is a second major decision for the next president. We need to think clearly about the magnitude of threat Al Qaeda and other terrorist groups pose for the U.S. and the international order, and revisit whether the means we are devoting to the effort are the right level and mix for countering radical Islamic extremism. Al Qaeda's attacks on the United States created an enormous systemic perturbation, diverting resources and effort in epic proportion from other priorities. After September 11, the Bush administration converted from realism to idealism, believing the United States could not be safe domestically unless other countries changed dramatically to embrace democracy as the cure for incipient terrorism. The record is at best mixed on whether promoting democracy has reduced terrorism, whether the magnitude of the threat merits the magnitude of effort the United States has expended, and whether a more consciously defensive strategy could better serve American interests. We have done a poor job of winning the war of ideas, although that should be our comparative advantage. More promising has been the insistence on holding states accountable for activity that emanates from within their borders.

Traditionally, American strategy is characterized by overwhelming problems with resources. Yet the Iraq War alone costs $2 billion a week, which should raise questions about the cost-effectiveness and sustainability of our strategy toward combating terrorism. There is little question America must keep fighting Al Qaeda and its virulent associates; what is less clear is whether the United States needs to lead a global effort against all terrorism. And if most terrorism has localized aims, political engagement to find solutions that isolate the forces of violence and address political issues by peaceful means might be a more productive approach than combating all terrorism as though it were Al Qaeda.

It will be tempting for the next president to make the popular choice of narrowing the scope of activity to uprooting Al Qaeda rather than combat terrorism more broadly. However, this would most likely lead to a more chaotic and violent international order. There would be large costs in increased volatility and reduced commerce, damaging both to the United States and to the global economy. The world would also be a worse place. Terrorism tends to migrate to poorly governed areas, further burdening the order's least capable states. While terrorism might not be paramount in those states' concerns, it aggravates their existing problems. Improving the quality of governance by engaging in localized political disputes while attacking the roots of terrorist activity continues to be a preferable approach for protecting and advancing American interests. Undertaking this effort successfully would require improving and expanding our diplomatic, law enforcement, educational, informational and other forms of engagement our government is not now resourced to provide.

Iraq. Surging American troops in Iraq to increase security in Baghdad and to provide Iraqi forces more time to organize and train has changed America's domestic debate about Iraq, demonstrating the sensitivity of public attitudes, not only to the cost of achieving objectives but also to the likelihood of success, and reducing the prospects of a precipitous withdrawal of American forces. Such a catastrophic end is not out of the question, however, especially if Iraqi political leaders remain incapable of making brave choices about the political structure and functioning of their country.

Whatever one thinks of the decision to invade Iraq, or of the Bush administration's management of the war, how the United States leaves Iraq will be a defining choice for the international order. If poorly managed, it will embolden challengers and be used as a justification by them for decades. A gradual reduction of troops as the Iraqi military forces gain competence and confidence continues to be the least costly approach. Political tracks to identify and further strengthen effective local leaders and cajole positive engagement by regional powers would also increase Iraq's prospects.

The outcome most damaging, both to Iraqis and to American power, would be the shattering of Iraq as a state. The advocates of threatening Iraqi political leaders with withdrawal have an understandable frustration that Iraqis are not working on the same timeline we are but gloss over our culpability in what would follow. The advocates of a "peaceful separation" strategy gloss over the forcible expulsions it would require and the long-term enmities it would engender, not to mention the temptation it would give to Iraq's neighbors to lay claims on territory.

The lessons of Iraq are not all negative for American power. The United States attacked a country believed to have weapons of mass destruction (WMD) with the intent of disarming it, creating a precedent that we would not be deterred from that kind of war. Despite being unprepared for the duration and cost of the war, the United States has continued to prosecute it longer than we fought World War II, showing that we will incur casualties and absorb costs for strategic objectives. The U.S. military is strained but has performed superbly and with restraint, adapting to changing circumstances. The economy has sustained the costs of the war while maintaining 5 percent growth and 4 percent unemployment. While some adversaries will surely be emboldened, there has not been a rash of preemptive attacks spuriously legitimized by the American National Security Strategy or from other challengers considering us vulnerable. Securing the international order has gotten marginally more expensive for the United States, but the long shadow of American power has not paled significantly because of Iraq.

Good government. The American government is poorly designed to centralize power, and purposely so, to the consternation of the earnest advocates of reforming the national security structures. The structure of American government is an enormous impediment in conducting policy, because it requires extraordinarily good management by the President's senior team to effectively orchestrate the tools the different departments can contribute to solving problems. Without good management, it reverts quickly to self-fulfilling bureaucracies. Even with good effort, the discrepancies in funding skew a president's ability to craft and execute strategies with integrated and time-sequenced effects.

The system has two fundamental problems: resourcing and responsibility. The U.S. government has a strategy requiring that many elements of state power be brought to bear on problems, but it hands departments an unfunded mandate. This means an underfunding of nondefense activity on the order of $80 billion, an amount that would bring other departments into line with the resources applied to defense. The next president can compensate somewhat by choosing superb managers to lead interagency coordination, but that cannot correct the inadequacy of non defense agencies without realigning resources.

The National Security Council ostensibly has authority for orchestrating and setting priorities in interagency activity. In most instances—not merely that of the Bush administration—the NSC has proved too weak to serve an integrating function. Radical proposals like deputizing the vice president to supervise interagency policy execution, authorizing a lead agency to take control of specific policies in their totality of means, or creating posts paralleling the relationships among military service chiefs and combatant commanders all have important drawbacks. A strategy that required less central control and instead emphasized loosely coordinated activity plays more to the strengths of American political culture.

In all likelihood, America will continue to operate with institutions cautiously designed to prevent the concentration of power rather than provide efficiency in policy making and execution. This outcome may be less than ideal, but it is the one most consistent with our political culture. If we are not going to improve the institutions, the system will continue to require exceptional and well-trained individuals to manage it effectively and will perform poorly without them.

If the next president were able to reduce U.S. debt, fight terrorism by helping states improve governance as well as attack terrorists, sustain support for continued involvement in Iraq until Iraqis are able to construct the foundations of a successful state, make the national security apparatus more consistently effective, he would dramatically strengthen the fundamentals of American power. Making choices that reduce the cost of sustaining American hegemony will alert futures traders of the money to be made buying on the rumor that American power will continue to dominate the international order.

★ ★ ★

AUTHOR'S NOTE: These essays were written before the U.S. changed course to adopt a counter-insurgency approach to the war in Iraq and also send additional forces commanders requested. That approach is now succeeding; violence is down 80% in Anbar province, once considered lost to the insurgency; Iraqi security forces are stepping forward to lead in securing their country; Iraqis are choosing to help us succeed; we have been able to turn over two-thirds of the provinces to Iraqi control; national leaders are making hard political choices because they are confident in our willingness to provide security.

The dramatic change in Iraq in the past 18 months illustrates many of the themes about the American cultural proclivity for problem solving, the strength and adaptiveness of the American military, and the under-resourcing of non-military parts of our strategy. The success of the surge now happily casts a very different light on the gloomy predictions for damage to America's power. It is to the smart people who figured out how to succeed in Iraq, had the heart to force a change in a losing strategy, and the strength and courage to see it through that this book is dedicated.

CHAPTER 1

Why Is American Power So Threatening?

★   ★   ★

American power was ascendant for most of the twentieth century, but fears about it seem to have taken on a qualitatively more anxious feel and quantitatively greater frequency in recent years. The end of the cold war freed up dread that previously had been focused on nuclear apocalypse or the spread of communism, and since the Soviet model had been vanquished, it is perhaps not surprising that some concern migrated to managing American hegemony. The United States was the last superpower standing, but it was quickly seen as much more: the only state in the international order with the ability to take action with impunity, to ignore international institutions, to insulate itself from the effects of other states' choices. We represent a fundamental asymmetry in the international order because the United States is seen as being unaffected by the actions of other states, whereas no state considers itself free of the effects of U.S. choices.

Concern about newly unrestrained power was not generalized to the West: the free market democracies ostensibly won the cold war, but concern has been about American power in the international order, not about Western power. Moreover, much of the concern expressed has come from America's closest allies, not its enemies. At times, America's enemies seem more accommodated to American power than its friends. This chapter explores why American power seems so intimidating to other states now, and what we can or should do about their concerns. The chapter focuses in particular on the European critique of American power, because the European states seem to have the least to fear from our hegemony: they are the preferred partners, the recipients of most of our diplomatic attention, the countries with the closest relationships with the United States and greatest influence over our choices, the ones we have bound ourselves to defend.

Several explanations have been posited for recent concern about American predominance: the decreasing legitimacy of American power; declining multilateralism by the United States; a recklessness particular to the Bush administration, compromising the goodwill of generations; changes in American political culture due to 9/11 that are difficult for longtime allies to appreciate; and even the "natural" proclivity of states to cooperate against a hegemon.

Legitimacy

When one speaks of legitimacy in international relations, what is meant is the acceptability of state actions to other states. "International law" is the fancy dress for what powerful states agree to in principle. As Shakespeare's Henry V says when his French fiancé refuses to kiss him because it is not the practice in her country, "nice customs curtsy to great kings, Kate. We are the makers of manners." So it is with powerful states and international law. States appeal to it to restrain others, but when a state's own interests are at stake, means of circumvention can usually be found. The illustrative post–cold war example is Kosovo, because it involves the states most committed to institutional constraint and international law, and because their motivation was commendable. The choice was a threefold intrusion into state rights by Europeans who champion the sole authority of the United Nations' remit in legitimating the use of force: their action lacked an authorizing resolution from the UN Security Council; it intruded into that most sacrosanct aspect of international law, the sovereign right of states to determine their domestic policies; and it posited a new standard for future international interventions, the prevention of harm to people by their own government. Europeans (and the United States) chose war in Kosovo because it was in their interest to stabilize the Balkans and because Serbian behavior so offended their morality. In the process Europeans legitimized the notion that there are "laws" higher than "international law": national interests and human rights.

Even in the tighter confines of powerful state norms as law, it is unclear what actions excepting the Iraq War (and the criticism predates

Iraq) the United States has taken after the end of the cold war so out of step with its earlier behavior as to call the legitimacy of our power into question. We fostered the peaceful reunification of Germany when Russia, France, and even the Thatcher government in Britain preferred to perpetuate its division.[1] We assisted the transition of former Warsaw Pact states to free market democracies, even taking on security guarantees for most of them. We did not demonize the Russians, but instead gave them the opportunity of a fresh start. We are largely supportive of rising powers, including China, while preventing their using force to subjugate others. We have encouraged an expanded role for Japan that does not threaten the interests of its neighbors. We have not prevented others from joining in cooperation that excludes us, whether in the European Union, the Association of Southeast Asian Nations (ASEAN), or the Shanghai Cooperation Organization. It would seem a pretty commendable record for a state with the ability to impose its will.

What Europeans seem to object to is the U.S.'s declining to join in cooperation that does not advance or protect our interests. We decline to accept that we need an international mandate for the use of force. We decline to accept that states can create "law" that binds other states without their consent, as in the International Criminal Court. We decline to become party to treaties, such as the Ottawa Land Mines Convention, that would prevent the carrying out of security obligations on terms we judge appropriate when we are not the cause of the problems those conventions seek to solve. We decline to consider treaties immutable when they contain provisions for parties to withdraw, as in the Anti-Ballistic Missile Treaty. These are attitudes of long standing in the U.S. political culture. They shouldn't be news, especially not to close allies.

Perhaps it is our own fault that other states believe there have been dramatic changes of direction in U.S. policies with the end of the cold war, since the largest perpetrators of that fiction are Americans themselves. We pretend new presidential administrations presage different approaches to foreign policy and talk as though they deliver on their promises of greater internationalism or tougher economic competition or "fair trade" when the swathe of agreement is quite wide on which

1. For a fantastic assessment of the Mitterrand and Thatcher governments' concerns about German unification, see Frederic Bozo, *Mitterrand, la fin de la guerre froide et l'unification allemande, De Yalta à Maastricht* (Odile Jacob, Paris, 2005).

problems we should engage in attempting to solve and what means are available to solve them.

If U.S. behavior has not substantially changed, perhaps norms in other states are transcending our practice to establish a higher, worthier standard of state behavior that we are failing to work up to. Perhaps other states fight their wars more justly and compromise their national interests for the greater good more easily. There is little evidence for that hypothesis, however. Other countries are not doing the hard work of advancing peace and security by means more virtuous than Americans have used. For the most part, they are simply not doing the work.

The United States is not behaving worse than other states in the international order. We are simply operating more, and under much greater scrutiny. The United States commits itself to protect more states and with more force than any other government would contemplate. American military forces in the wars we are fighting in Afghanistan and Iraq are operating with greater restraint under fire and greater concern for civilian populations than virtually any other military in the world could achieve.

It is true that other militaries operate with greater cultural knowledge and sensitivity than the U.S. military does, and our limitations in this regard often result in greater resentment of our presence or a higher price in casualties. But often this criticism ignores three important countervailing forces. First, U.S. forces are more attractive targets for insurgent forces than are most countries' militaries, because we generally lead the operations we participate in, and therefore derailing U.S. involvement would collapse the operation. Second, military training is a full-time occupation in contemporary warfare, and there are operational trade-offs to spending training time on noncombat skills. Third, because of the global security obligations of the United States, our military cannot afford to specialize in the way expansive cultural awareness requires. We cannot devote ourselves to becoming Arabists because we must also be Sinologists and South Asianists and Hispanologists. U.S. military forces run different risks than other militaries do, and have a broader range of obligations, even before addressing the American insistence on retaining a war-winning (as opposed to a peacekeeping) military. We can, and should, build awareness of the environments in which our forces operate, but expecting the American military to optimize to the needed skills would simply increase the likelihood that the United States would not intervene.

Besides, securing the international order is not simply a popularity contest. Our government's responsibility is the well-being of the American people. That our choices are unpopular may say more about the states objecting than about the nefariousness of our actions. The easy cases are Iran's objecting to our nonproliferation activities, North Korea's decrying our approach to government accountability, or Middle Eastern authoritarian governments' disclaiming our support for democracy movements. In those cases, the governments all have a strong interest in undercutting U.S. policies. But those are not the critics that gain traction. The critics that gain traction are European critics.

Multilateralism

When Europeans complain about the declining legitimacy of U.S. international involvement, they mean either that we are not doing what they want us to do, or we are not doing it through the institutions they value. Consultations with Europeans are near constant and take up far and away the majority of U.S. diplomatic engagement: we consult with Europeans bilaterally, both in their capitals and in Washington, through NATO and the European Union, at the United Nations. It cannot be that the quantity of consulting is insufficient; what Europeans are really complaining about is that U.S. policies are insufficiently malleable to their influence. We are unilateral if we do not adopt common transatlantic policies.

The rallying cry against U.S. unilateralism rings from nearly every underused European church bell tower, but in truth the United States rarely acts alone. The complaint really translates to the United States' not accepting European vetoes. When the United States was unable to achieve a UN Security Council resolution for invading Iraq, it received public endorsement of the war from fifty-six other countries—a much more significant international validation than the fifteen members of the Security Council represent. When the United States invaded Iraq, it did so with military forces from thirty-seven other countries—one-fifth of the world's countries validated the war by their own participation.[2] Thirty-nine other countries have declined to sign the international convention banning land mines, not coincidentally most of those with extensive or difficult to defend land borders.[3] Yet when the United States is criticized for not joining the treaty, what is gleefully reported is that we are in the company of North Korea, Iran, and Cuba.

Perhaps the most resented American refusal is of the Kyoto Treaty restricting greenhouse gas emissions, since the United States is now the largest producer of that pollutant. Even in that case, the 141 signatories account for only 51 percent of total global emissions, and the states likely to produce much greater quantities as their economies develop also chose not to participate. In each celebrated case of the United States' declining to participate in international undertakings, we have not acted alone, even if we have not acted through international institutions.

The constraints of international institutions work most effectively when either the basic agreement on rules and policies is broad (as on security in NATO or social policies in the European Union), or when achieving an outcome supersedes in importance the substance of the outcome (as, for most states, in Palestine). The UN is simply incapable of dealing with crises affecting the most powerful states because these states control its outcomes. It is impossible to imagine the UN playing a useful role in punishing Russia for using energy supplies to blackmail former Soviet states. Even a regional power like Iran can be *in flagrante delicto* with regard to the UN Security Council's demand that it cease uranium enrichment, to little effect. The UN is incapable of moving against the interests of the strongest states; it can only withhold support from the strong and punish the weak (if they are not shielded by one of the strong). The UN is mostly useful for making a public case of dangerous behavior against another state to raise the cost of such behavior by shaping international attitudes. In sum, the UN is an imperfect tool for managing international peace and security, and certainly not the *deus ex machina* of virtuous international action.

The UN tends to get problems dumped on it either because they

2. For listings of those countries, see Global Security coalition update, http://www.globalsecur ity.org/military/ops/iraq_orbat_coalition.htm.

3. These states include China, Russia, Finland, Egypt, India, Pakistan, South Korea, Saudi Arabia. For a complete list, see http://www.icbl.org/treaty/snp.

are intractable (Israel-Palestine) or states don't care enough to solve the problem nationally (genocide in Darfur). Those critical of the UN record in producing good outcomes should weight the grade of its performance by these two factors. While deference for the United Nations is most everywhere higher than in the United States, the "international institutions create legitimacy" argument overstates the extent to which states adjudicate their gravest concerns through international institutions. For example, perhaps no state trumpets the importance of the United Nations in international peace and security as fervently as Germany does, but Germany never permitted a UN role in the Berlin crises or in adjudication of its national unification, and fought in Kosovo without UN sanction. Europeans are perhaps more enthusiastic about UN legitimation because their own security problems seem distant at this time.

Why, then, do Europeans treat the UN as the seminal legitimizing body? Europeans have a greater affinity for institutions that orchestrate international activity than does the United States. As small- and medium-sized states, they seldom believe acting alone will achieve their objectives. Small- and medium-sized states have better odds of restraining the strongest states through agreed practices and institutional power sharing; the strongest states have an interest in the validation of multilateralism. It should match. But most states do not entrust their security, economies, or domestic policies to international institutions. The countries of the European Union are unique in the extent to which they pool sovereignty for common policies; what is extraordinary is the extent to which they believe the EU experience is a microcosm for the international order.

Another weakness of the institutional argument is that it overstates the extent to which the United States has ever been committed to institutions. The NATO commitment is unique in American experience, our promise to our closest friends in the world at the end of a savage war and with a bristling threat near to them; NATO correspondingly is the international institution with the highest level of U.S. support. We have always had a strong strain of domestic concern about participating in the UN, much less binding our policies to its proscriptions. It is of substantial value to the United States to have UN validation of its action, but we fought long wars in Vietnam and Iraq and invaded Panama and Grenada without the benefit of UN approval. Approval from the NATO nations has the strongest legitimating value of any international institution, and yet NATO also has never served to restrain the United States from using military force.

The institutional legitimacy argument is most vociferously advanced by Europeans and Europeanists; not surprisingly, since European states are the ones with the greatest success in constraining American power through institutions and have expended such enormous effort in constructing the European Union among themselves. We have mostly agreed on security in Europe and given wide latitude to European concerns about whether and how wars would be fought. This was proper, as the war would be fought on their territories. Yet even in those circumstances, the United States retained a separate, national chain of command to take unilateral action. And despite all the ties that bind the United States to Europe institutionally, we have never really agreed on security issues outside of Europe. The United States strongly supported decolonization in the 1940s and 1950s; refused assistance to the British, French, and Israeli attack on Suez in 1956; fought a decade in Vietnam without European assistance; and supported insurgents in Central America in the 1980s over European objections. It is difficult now to imagine Europeans fighting to defend Taiwan from China, as the United States has committed to do, or redoubling their involvement in Iraq because of our troubles there.

Disagreement on security issues outside Europe is not new in the transatlantic relationship. What is new is the expectation on the part of the Europeans that the special relationships and institutional restraints the United States accepted as reasonable when defense of European homelands was at stake are exportable to other problems and other regions. European governments, and European publics, seem to take for granted that as their views on defending Europe have disproportionate influence in U.S. policymaking, their views on all issues should. From an American perspective, this is not obviously the case. Europeans assume an Olympian legitimacy in their own participation. It is unclear to many Americans why, say, a Greek veto in NATO should carry weight when genocide in Darfur is the issue, or why Belgian concerns about Iraq should be more important than those of countries more directly affected by, or taking responsibility to help with, those crises. Secretary Rumsfeld's description of "a coalition of the willing" was certainly resented in Europe, but it seems obvious for many Americans that countries willing to shoulder burdens are the countries whose views are most important in decision making.

Retaliating for the September 11 attack is illustrative of the current friction in our alliance relationships. Europeans stood in reassuring solidarity with the United States after the attacks, invoking NATO's mutual defense clause for the first time in the alliance's history, working capably and cooperatively to close U.S. airspace and international financial markets and bring about the UN Security Council resolution authorizing the use of force against the Taliban in Afghanistan. Vigils at the German Bundestag and Buckingham Palace and by friendly ships at sea strengthened us, as did George Robertson, NATO's eloquent and pugnacious secretary general, saying "they have had their Pearl Harbor, but we shall have our Tokyo Bay."[4] The British government once again played the role that makes our relationship so special: quickly assessing the crisis, privately telling the U.S. government what needed doing, and outlining what they had underway to bring it into being. Even the French mourned with us, *Le Monde* declaring "we are all Americans now."[5]

As the United States moved from mourning to retribution, however, the tenor of transatlantic conversations changed. Europeans were genuinely surprised that the United States would give the command of the military operation to U.S. Central Command (CENTCOM) rather than NATO, as though regional expertise, personal relationships with military leaders in the region, and familiarity with existing military plans and assigned forces were of less value in the fight than a commander knowledgeable of Europeans. The speed and innovation in operations would likewise exclude meaningful participation by most European militaries unless the United States committed significant effort to underwriting their participation, diverting both resources and attention from a difficult military challenge. The United States might even be forgiven wanting a show of national strength after such a painful revelation of our vulnerabilities. Europeans talk woundedly of having offered assistance that was not taken, seldom acknowledging the limits on what they could practically contribute. They complain of having been in the coalition

4. George Robertson, "An Attack on Us All: NATO's Response to Terrorism," (Atlantic Council of the United States, October 10, 2001).

5. Jean-Marie Colombani, *Le Monde,* Sept. 12, 2001, *World Press Review* 48, no. 11 (Nov. 2001).

trailer park at CENTCOM headquarters (instead of in more prestigious digs than those offered to non-NATO contributors), and of the United States' not having incorporated their diplomatic expertise in the region. To summarize, even in our greatest recent national trauma, Europeans wanted us to worry about their concerns, to give them status superior to that of others, to tackle their problems, to enable them to play the role their own capabilities did not. This is not to say that the United States made a terrific choice in not finding useful activity for Europeans to contribute to in the aftermath of September 11. It is only to suggest that while the shock of September 11 was still fresh, perhaps a solipsistic America might be cut a little slack by a solipsistic Europe.

The Bush Factor

Europeans have an overwhelming antipathy for President Bush. He seems to represent all they fear about American power and the undeservingness of American society to sit ignorantly and inattentively atop the international order. The undignified scramble of the 2000 election prevented Europeans from connecting our public to the president. His reelection in 2004 over a candidate far more comfortable to European sensibilities frightened Europeans with the specter of an America that would choose George Bush to lead, after a first term and therefore knowing what he is. The superb public opinion polls of the German Marshall Fund capture the effect of this disillusionment: from 2003 to 2008 the negative attitudes about American power or the U.S. government had the caveat of not applying to the American people; since 2004, attitudes have been anti-American with no distinction between the government and its people.[6]

But is America really different under the Bush administration? Or were previous administrations simply more polite in representing the continuities of American policies? As difficult as it now is to conjure up thinking about security between 1991 and the cataclysmic effect of September 11, 2001, by the late 1990s there was already a substantial di-

6. German Marshall Fund of the United States, Transatlantic Trends (polling conducted every six months), http://www.transatlantictrends.org/trends.

vergence in transatlantic perspectives on security. Europeans were understandably focused on integrating the newly democratic states into Europe and stabilizing the Balkans. American defense experts were debating "asymmetric" challenges to our conventional supremacy: weapons of mass destruction (WMD), terrorism, information warfare.[7] Innovations in American military practice were already being driven by the demands of new challenges, and policymakers were confronting the complexities of attempting to deter and punish terrorist acts.

Attacks on American embassies in Kenya and Tanzania that killed 312 people and injured 5,000 in August of 1998 appear in retrospect to be the seminal turning point of American policy. The Clinton administration traced the embassy attacks to Al Qaeda, and retaliated with military strikes on Afghanistan and the Sudan. In justifying the attacks, President Clinton said, "Our target was the terrorists' base of operation and infrastructure. Our objective was to damage their capacity to strike at Americans and other innocent people."[8] That is, the purpose of using military force was not only punitive but also preemptive—to prevent future harm.

Later the same day President Clinton expounded further on U.S. motives, saying that the facilities were attacked in both Afghanistan and Sudan "because of the imminent threat they presented to our national security." In words that could easily be ascribed to his successor, President Clinton said:

> Our mission was clear—to strike at the network of radical groups affiliated with and funded by Osama bin Laden, perhaps the preeminent organizer and financier of international terrorism in the world today. The groups associated with him come from diverse places, but share a hatred for democracy, a fanatical glorification of violence, and a horrible distortion of their religion to justify the murder of innocents. They have made the United States their adversary precisely because of what we stand for and what we stand against.[9]

7. See, for example, Lloyd J. Matthews, ed., *Challenging the United States Symmetrically and Asymmetrically: Can America Be Defeated?* (U.S. Army War College Strategic Studies Institute, July 1998).

8. Statement by President Clinton, Edgartown Elementary School, August 20, 1998.

9. Address to the nation by President Clinton, the Oval Office, August 20, 1998.

President Clinton also linked Al Qaeda to killing American, Belgian, and Pakistani peacekeepers in Somalia, plotting to assassinate the president of Egypt and the Pope, planning to bomb six U.S. airliners over the Pacific, bombing the Egyptian embassy in Pakistan, and killing German tourists in Egypt.

The president stated that the United States had for years warned the governments of Afghanistan and Sudan to cease harboring and supporting terrorist groups, and that "countries that persistently host terrorists have no right to be safe havens." To state the idea somewhat differently, the right of states to sovereignty in the international order is contingent on their exercising their power responsibly—exercising it in a way consistent with our security.

He closed the address to the nation by saying "the risks from inaction to America and the world would be far greater than action, for that would embolden our enemies, leaving their ability and their willingness to strike us intact." These are the exact arguments that animate the Bush administration's 2002 National Security Strategy.

Clinton's address represented an extraordinary and sweeping shift in American strategy, all the more so for having drawn almost no negative response from Europeans. The British government defended the attack, including the strike on the Al Shifa pharmaceutical plant in Sudan. The Arab League and Islamic Conference condemned the attacks, but Arab governments were silent. The United Nations declined the Sudanese government's offer to inspect the site for chemical weapons residue (the United States had refused to reveal the intelligence on which the targeting was based, and was generally criticized for faulty intelligence). The *Economist* mildly suggested that "America's counter-terrorist air strikes on August 20th may turn out to have been unwise."[10]

Which is not to say the Bush administration's response was either the only or even the right one. There are many possible strategies for dealing with a world of terrorist threats: focus on improving situational awareness to prevent attacks; refuse to divert resources from other activities, accepting as the cost of doing business that occasionally an attack will succeed; improve international legal frameworks to deal with terrorism

10. "Punish and Be Damned," *Economist,* August 27, 1998.

as a law enforcement issue; redouble efforts to defang the local political grievances on which most terrorist movements gain legitimacy.

Not surprisingly, the Bush administration chose an aggressive response—not only in retaliating against Al Qaeda and overthrowing the Taliban regime but also in the considered development of doctrine for an age of terrorism that became the 2002 National Security Strategy. The new strategy emphasized the "perilous crossroads of radicalism and technology," the evaporation of warning time and magnitude of resources that formerly characterized the requirements for wars against great powers, the futility of containment or attempts to win on the defensive.[11] In retrospect, the strategy sounds frightened, a reminder to ourselves that the United States has means to bring order to a world of terrifying new developments and can take comfort in commencing the work. However, the 2002 National Security Strategy (NSS) does not depart in dramatic ways from the Clinton administration's decisions in 1998.

Nor was it so radical a vision that the European Union's high representative, Javier Solana, would rebut those elements in the European Security Strategy (ESS) the following year.[12] In fact, the ESS refined and extended the NSS arguments in ways that increased their palatability for European audiences without changing their fundamental nature. The policy implications of Europe's new strategy were also outlined: "we need to develop a strategic culture that fosters early, rapid, and when necessary, robust intervention." While member governments did not formally adopt the ESS and it remained untested whether they would commit resources and shoulder responsibilities commensurate with the strategy's direction, the ESS suggested that the governments on both sides of the Atlantic largely agreed on the threats and were converging in their approaches in the aftermath of September 11.[13]

One decision the Bush administration made that was crucially different from what any Democratic—or even different Republican— administration would probably have made is pivoting so quickly to

11. President George Bush, West Point commencement address, June 1, 2002.

12. Solana, *A Secure Europe in a Better World* (Brussels: The Council of the European Union, December 12, 2003).

13. This is the conclusion of the German Marshall Fund's 2003 Transatlantic Trends report.

attack Iraq. Democrats argue, persuasively even if self-servingly, that a Gore administration would have remained focused on uprooting Al Qaeda and stabilizing Afghanistan, would not have characterized vanquishing terrorism as a global war or spurned allied offers of assistance, and would not have dealt with the erosion of Iraq containment by overthrowing the Saddam Hussein government. These pious improvements on history are most likely true. However, it is possible to imagine the course evolving in largely the same way even under Democratic leadership: the administration lambasted for being soft on terrorism and for using only pinprick strikes to handle a problem that required ground forces; investigations by a Republican-controlled Congress in which Dick Clarke accused the administration of doing too little despite his best efforts to alert them to the growing Al Qaeda threat; the White House feeling the need to respond to voters' yearning for no-nonsense law and order and not wanting to risk the greater casualties or diminished military effectiveness of operating in a coalition; the administration consumed with worry about emboldened enemies and where the next threat would emerge, and facing a chorus of criticism for allowing our so-called allies to unravel any substantive constraint on Iraq's WMD programs and for not having a policy for how to fix the problem. An inverse of the Nixon to China phenomenon might well have occurred in which a Democratic administration needed to look even tougher on terrorism than its Republican counterpart did.

A Different America

If the world looked dangerous to Americans before 9/11, it certainly felt dramatically more so after the attacks. The United States really is different afterwards—lonelier—in ways that alarm many Europeans, even long-time friends of this country. The attacks on New York and Washington have made the United States feel like a hegemon: powerful, targeted, and fundamentally alone.

It is difficult to overstate the fear of another attack in the immediate aftermath of September 11. Senior people in the administration worried they had not done enough, and had failed to protect the American people. They feared a more spectacular attack to follow from Al Qaeda or other origins, involving nuclear or chemical or biological weapons.

The search for emerging threats focused on Iraq because of the games Saddam Hussein was playing with UN weapons inspectors. Whatever else one may say about Iraq, Saddam Hussein worked very hard to convince the international community that he had weapons of mass destruction and had bought enough influence in the UN Security Council that it would nonetheless allow sanctions to expire.

The Bush administration desperately did not want to go back to Americans after another attack and explain that we'd known Saddam Hussein was a problem for fifteen years; that we'd fought a war against him and were sufficiently worried even after we won that we took a third of his country out of his control and kept continuous military operations underway in both the north and south of Iraq; that Saddam Hussein had not only developed chemical weapons and used them on Iran during their war but had also used chemical weapons against his own population, and that we'd stood impotently sentinel while the international community allowed any meaningful constraints on his weapons programs to evaporate. Add to that a growing sense that the political climate of the Middle East was poisonous, radicalizing, and likely to keep producing terrorists unless a dramatic change occurred. For a country traumatized by recent attack, it is a more reasonable path to war than our polarized debate about the Iraq War captures. It is not inconceivable that a different American administration, even a Democratic administration, might have even made the same choice.

But acrimony over Iraq unquestionably shattered the picture of common approaches on force and legitimacy across the Atlantic. Not only did Europe split over the appropriateness of attacking Iraq, but the Bush administration added insult to injury by caricaturing "old Europe" as unwilling to defend common security.[14] While offensive, Secretary Rumsfeld's insult was not wholly inaccurate in its acknowledgement of the differing underlying approaches to handling emergent threats. There was, and remains, a stark difference between U.S. attitudes and those of aggregate "Europe" in their support for the use of force.[15] The German Marshall Fund's survey Transatlantic Trends measures the difference to be roughly 30 percent. Moreover, in the United States, support for the

14. "Outrage at Old Europe Remarks" (BBC, January 23, 2003).
15. Robert Kagan captured the divergent perspectives in *Of Paradise and Power* (New York: Alfred A. Knopf, 2003).

use of military force is largely unaffected by the conditions in which force is used. That is, the level does not fluctuate whether the United States would use force unilaterally or multilaterally, with or without a UN or other international institution's mandate.[16]

Another crucial transatlantic difference is the backlash to not finding weapons of mass destruction in Iraq. President Bush does not really suffer politically from being wrong on the basis for the war. His approval ratings before September 11 were in the high 40s; after September 11 they shot dramatically up to 88 percent until the middle of 2002, at which time they stabilized in the mid-60s. The president's approval spiked with the invasion of Iraq and did not drop consistently below 50 percent, its pre–9/11 level, until 2005.[17] The president's negatives did rise after the invasion of Iraq, but support for his policies remained consistent for almost two years despite the lack of proof of his argument for war. In fact, the president suffered public disapproval for having handled the use of force ineptly, not for having fought the war, even under unproven pretenses.

By contrast, the Blair government was ruined by being wrong on weapons of mass destruction, even though the prime minister had also made the argument for humanitarian intervention forcefully and over time.[18] Nearly every European government that supported the invasion of Iraq was voted from power, and all have seen Iraq subsume the rest of their political agendas. It is true that many governments supported the invasion for reasons of their relationship with the United States, rather than the WMD case against Iraq, but the costs to them in public support and perceived legitimacy for using force have been staggering.

American risk tolerance has shifted because of the September 11 attacks. A president can afford to be wrong in the direction of doing too much to protect us, but he or she cannot afford to be wrong in doing too little. Given the magnitude of difference between the United States and Europe in public attitudes and government requirements, is a transatlantic approach to using force re-creatable? To put the question another

---

16. Transatlantic Trends, p. 11.

17. These figures are from the Harris Poll, http://www.pollingreport.com/BushJob1.htm.

18. Prime Minister Blair's Chicago Economic Club speech in April of 1999 remains the most powerful argument for the responsibility for humanitarian interventions.

way: if it weren't for the Bush administration, would Europeans support the United States? Many European elites have fostered the belief that the transatlantic fractiousness on issues of war is attributable to their dislike of and disdain for the Bush administration. While it may be true in magnitude, it seems unlikely to be true in type. European governments did not protest the Clinton administration's taking unilateral military action against two sovereign states in 1998, nor did they contest the assertion by the administration that the strikes were both punitive and preemptive. However, they did not participate. European governments did not object to Solana's European Security Strategy mirroring the 2002 National Security Strategy in its important elements. However, they did not formally approve the strategy or take action on the basis of its precepts. European governments may consider Iraq a unique event, but the sifting of national risk tolerance evident in Iraq is also playing out in Afghanistan, where the operation was mandated by the United Nations and undertaken by NATO as part of its mutual security clause. The French government may complain that the United States is undercutting European negotiations with Iran on its nuclear program by "not acting like the United States" (e.g., not overtly threatening to attack Tehran's nuclear sites). However, Europeans are not threatening to attack Tehran when their individual and combined military strength are adequate to serve the same purpose. A real closing of the gap in perspectives is unlikely, which should lead us to question whether we are overinvested in European relationships and should explore other alliances that might provide a closer match with our perspective on the work that needs doing in the international order.

Restraining Gulliver

Political scientists in international relations formulate general theories about state behavior. It is, as George Quester has said, "history with an argument." Realism (a school of thought meriting our consideration for having named itself so advantageously) argues essentially that all states behave in the same way; they seek power and autonomy, principally by using threats of force. For realists, the particularities of history, culture, governmental structure, and individual leaders are marginal factors in determining state behavior. Taken to the extreme, their argument would consider Hitler's Germany indistinguishable in its choices from Churchill's Britain.

The spoiler of realist theory is often the United States, because our behavior is more idealistic than their paradigm can account for. Explaining American generosity toward vanquished Germany and Japan in 1945, or support for democracy movements and human rights, requires contortions from realists. It overstates the case to say, as the admirable Colin Powell has, that the United States is the only country that has never sought territory except as cemetaries to bury its fallen.[19] At least, that would come as a surprise to Mexico, which was forced in war to cede a third of its territory to us, or the Philippines, or Canada, which even now fears absorption of its provinces into the United States.[20] Realists accumulate a depressingly large body of evidence for U.S. foreign policy being just an expression of our power rather than exemplifying our values. But in our defense, we can say that at our finest, the United States has not only believed but often shown that our interests and our values can both be accommodated in enlightened foreign policies.

The United States is not the only state with behavior at odds with realism: the most prominent contemporary advocate of the theory, John Mearsheimer, famously and inaccurately predicted that a unified Germany would become aggressively independent on security issues, and acquire nuclear weapons to threaten other states.[21]

Even with its gaffes, realism is sensibly the theory of first resort. That is, knowing nothing about a situation, your best bet in approximating the reason for a state's behavior would be positing that it is seeking to increase its power and autonomy. Other theories, in order to determine outcomes, require substantially more information about the history, culture, kind of government, or institutional participation of states. Also,

19. Secretary of State Colin L. Powell, "Address Upon Receiving the Dwight David Eisenhower Distinguished Service Award and Citation" (Cincinnati, VFW, Aug. 16, 2004).

20. The U.S. Information Agency, which used to be an independent arm of the State Department (rather as the Marine Corps is to the navy) found in 1992 that the number one national security fear of Canadians was that their Meech Lake Accords would fail to contain Quebecois separatism and provinces would become U.S. states. The same poll had the delightful insight to determine that more Canadians believed they had seen Elvis alive than believed their prime minister was doing his job well.

21. John Mearsheimer, "Back to the Future: Instability in Europe After the Cold War," *International Security* 15, no. 4 (Summer 1990): pp. 5–56.

their predictive record is not demonstrably stronger. History has a tendency toward unique events. American hegemony in the international order with the end of the cold war is just such a unique event. Its closest parallel is the dominance of Rome at the height of its empire, but even that falls considerably short of the breadth of American power at the turn of the twenty-first century.[22]

Realism predicts an eventual ganging up by all other states against the hegemon. The theory considers hegemony inherently unstable, with other powers cooperating to prevent the strongest from achieving its goals until it is whittled down to a more equal status with that of other states. But this assumes that what the hegemon wants is naturally objectionable to other states, when the genius of American power in the twentieth century has been setting and enforcing rules of participation by which all who opt into the system can be successful. Because realism leaves no room for the particularities of states, it has no way to assess that our power may be less—or more—offensive than others', and therefore hegemony more sustainable for us than for other states.

One of the particularities of America is that culturally we want to be liked in the world. Realism has never vanquished the more idealist theories because they capture the desire to be a force for good that motivates critical elements in American politics. Because international engagement has been a luxury rather than a necessity for the United States throughout much of our history—we have nearly always viewed our wars as wars of choice rather than compulsion—choosing to help fix other people's problems has an evangelical component for American foreign policy. The historian Arnold Toynbee best described the question of American power for other states: "America is like a large, friendly dog in a very small room: it wants so much to please you that it starts wagging its tail and knocks all the furniture over."[23]

The signs of other states in the international order banding together to restrain American power, much as Jonathan Swift's Lilliputians subdued Gulliver, are scant. The four examples that trend most in that direction are: the establishment of the International Criminal Court (ICC), France's

---

22. For an excellent review of comparative power, see Elliot Cohen, "History and the Hyperpower," *Foreign Affairs* (July/August 2004).

23. Arnold Toynbee (July 14, 1954), quoted in *Simpson's Contemporary Quotations* (New York: Houghton Mifflin, 1988), p. 5404.

attempt to build a coalition against the Iraq War, the Russian organization of the Shanghai Cooperation Organization, and Hugo Chavez' efforts to help anti-American leaders gain power in Latin America.

The main reason the International Criminal Court treaty serves as an example is that unlike other treaties under which states can merely choose not to participate, the ICC accrues to itself the right to impose its law on states without their consent. The United States participated in negotiations over founding the ICC and expected to accede to the treaty. The United States was concerned about the potential for politicized trials of American military men and women, even the possibility of senior government officials being brought before the court; because of the expansive security commitments the United States has undertaken, such trials represented a serious potential liability. European negotiators believed the treaty's inclusion of a right of first refusal by states to try offenders was adequate protection, refused compromise, and were stunned when the Clinton administration refused to sign the treaty. Later efforts by the Bush administration to deny military assistance to states that do not indemnify the United States against military personnel being turned over to the ICC were probably counterproductive, given the multiplicity of means the United States has to prevent such outcomes, and were eventually discontinued.

The ICC represents the first attempt by other states to impose their collective will on the United States. The effort was unsuccessful, partly because for the ICC to really function, it would need to depend on the provision of intelligence information and assistance by the United States, and partly because the principal advocates of the court continue to rely on U.S. activism to secure the international order. The most vociferous advocates of the ICC would not have thought to enforce its dictates against the colossus of American power. They might proceed without us, as the court did, carefully selecting cases the United States would support prosecuting, and hoping we would grow comfortable with a standing international tribunal.

The Chirac government's effort in 2003 to rally opposition to the U.S. invasion of Iraq represents a unilateral challenge to American power. Its opening gambit was using a French-sponsored UN meeting on terrorism to castigate the U.S. arguments for war in Iraq. When it became clear that the French and German governments could not stitch together a unified EU opposition, President Chirac sought support from a gathering of French-speaking countries. In the end the United States lacked the votes in the Security Council to force a French (or possibly Russian) veto, but France made little progress toward the multipolarity it was striking poses about: fifty-six countries openly supported the U.S. invasion, and military forces of thirty-six countries participated. The French alternative, in retrospect, had the ability to deny the United States a Security Council resolution but not to prevent the United States from taking action or having a considerable measure of international support. Moreover, it did not brand France as nobly virtuous, a rising power worth risking your country's fortunes alongside, or strong enough to be a counterweight to the United States. France has a unique ability to irritate, when the United States will pay attention, and often takes positions others clandestinely favor but are unwilling to own up to. But France lacks the benefits at its disposal and the likeability or intimidation of a genuine challenger to American hegemony.

Russia, China, Kazakhstan, Kyrgyzstan, and Uzbekistan founded the Shanghai Cooperation Organization (SCO) in 2001 as a confidence-building measure along disputed borders. Although the SCC has no mutual defense pledge, the Russian government often trumpets it as an alternative NATO and suggests that SCC countries will move into intelligence sharing and military cooperation. The SCC did implicitly suggest in July of 2005 that U.S. forces should not be stationed in the region, though U.S. support for democratic revolutions in the Ukraine and Georgia and American criticism of Uzbekistan's crackdown on demonstrations had already made the cessation of U.S. basing likely. There are suggestions Iran may join the group, but the SCC does not appear a promising start on creating an anti-American alliance: first, because the burgeoning U.S.-China relationship offers much more opportunity for the Chinese, and second, because other states are unlikely to want the Russians setting rules for economic or political activity, given the ominous trends by Moscow in those areas.

Venezuelan President Hugo Chavez has a flair for fiery rhetoric (his UN General Assembly speech decrying George Bush as the devil should not be missed). He also has the benefit of the world's sixth-largest oil deposits and a seeming commitment to supporting anti-American governments in Latin America. His "Bolivarian revolution" embraces Cuba's

Fidel Castro, both literally and in antipathy to free markets and democratic government. Chavez has been profligate, buying 100,000 rifles from Russia, offering Cuba $400 million in aid, and funding expansion of the Panama Canal. Because of the history of American corporate and government behavior in Latin America, there would seem to be fertile ground for progress. In fact, the U.S. government is concerned about a Bolivarian alternative, especially coming at a time when the euphoria of democratic transition in Latin American countries has given way to the grinding difficulties of institutionalizing reform and developing economies to keep pace with public expectations. The takers are actually surprisingly few, considering what Chavez has on offer.

As to states banding together to contain American power, it could be, as Chou En-Lai said in evaluating the success of the French revolution, "it's too soon to tell." Other better-organized groups with the right membership could emerge to impose their will on the United States. But there is little evidence, fifteen years after the end of the cold war, that such a bloc is emerging. The benefits of opting into the American model are so great, and the exercise of American power sufficiently tolerable to most states in the international order, that we are likelier to end up as Gulliver in Laputa (the island kingdom of impractical intellectuals) with our allies than in Lilliput.

Totemic America

None of the explanations for the intensity of concern by our closest friends—that the legitimacy of U.S. power has irrecoverably waned, that we are unwilling to consign our choices to international institutions, that President Bush is so polarizing a figure, that America has changed in response to the shock of the September 11 attacks, and that states are ganging up against the United States as they would any other—ring fully true. They sound more like rationalizations than reasons. They also set up standards that, if we adopted them, would dramatically proscribe U.S. international behavior. They want us never to be wrong; and the only way to achieve that is never to act. But this view fails to weigh the moral consequences of doing nothing: one can be equally wrong for failing to act.

We should be honored that our friends want to hold us to so high a standard: that they think we are capable of complying shows that we remain a City on a Hill. But it is also true that we have taken on graver obligations than most other states, and after the end of the cold war, most European states have not yet broadened the horizon of their international commitments beyond Europe. The responsibilities the United States has for securing the international order do often give us a different perspective on problems. Even if the American people would accept a U.S. foreign policy constrained by the need to achieve international consensus through existing institutions while being consistently popular and not electing leaders that frighten the rest of the world, it would leave the international order more dangerously exposed.

The same spread of technology and commerce that has enriched us as globalization advances has enabled the spread of weapons that once only a wealthy, powerful state could acquire. Thus weapons are not only proliferating, but it is increasingly difficult for states to know when threats are building. Resentful countries like Iran and Russia, which believe they deserve status they have been denied, are taking advantage of the hesitancy of states and frailty of international institutions. Weak countries like North Korea are threatening damage for reasons difficult to comprehend. Globalization is making it more difficult for governments to shield their societies from ideas that challenge existing social structures and comfortable traditions. Expectations are rising from the vulgar (latinate for the common people), who are choosing those very things their leaders can't provide or want to prevent them having.

Europeans, and many others, are afraid of our power because they are afraid of the ways the international order is changing and lack confidence in their ability to shape those changes. As a result, they become inordinately protective of an eroding status quo. Our friends, so recently relieved of the burden of the cold war, don't want an international order this frightening. And they believe we are creating it.

CHAPTER 2

Globalization as Americanization

* * *

One of the ironies about the age of globalization is that globalization is considered by many an American phenomenon. Outside the United States, our country is seen as causing globalization. To Americans, it appears a neutral phenomenon we are harnessing to advantage; to many others, it appears an insurmountable juggernaut of American political, economic, military, cultural, and linguistic power against which other cultures cannot shield themselves. Certainly a main reason would be that we are an early beneficiary of this round of globalization, but the explanation is insufficient to account for the seething resentment "Americanization" often incurs. After all, the greatest beneficiaries, as Amartya Sen persuasively argues, have been the world's poor, most of whom are not American.[1]

Those concerned about globalization equate it strongly with the United States. They may be wrong, in which case other states or non-state actors will surpass the power and influence of the United States. Our early lead will prove ephemeral, and the perception be corrected. It is certainly the hope of most U.S. competitors and even U.S. allies that "the unipolar moment" has passed, and the United States will be sized down to a scale in which it is not immune to influence. Other countries will broadcast news we all watch, other economies will grow wealthier and set the terms of trade, other societies will successfully imitate our achievements or will produce nimbler ways to solve problems, other governments will be preferred partners. *Sic transit gloria mundi,* America will become what other great empires became in their twilight, either

1. Amartya Sen, *Development As Freedom* (Oxford University Press, 2001).

declining gracefully or violently struggling to retain its diminishing power.

Alternatively, our early shaping of globalization may have introduced structural rigidities, even into a globalizing international order, that can not be overcome. For example, American English with its soft consonants and, in Barbara Hamby's lovely phrase, "mongrel plenitude," may have become the equivalent of the QWERTY typewriter keyboard, perpetuated internationally long after outliving the purpose of its standardization.[2] Having the *lingua franca,* Wall Street and Hollywood may prove insurmountable advantages for the United States simply because they existed earlier than their competitors did. The large-scale interaction of globalization requires a standardization of infrastructure that advantages early arrivers: common electrical plugs, the international date line, and the Gregorian calendar have all proved remarkably durable. The need to establish a standard, even when not ideal, that permits predictability is of enormous value for efficiency in large-scale enterprises like globalization. However, as extinction of the eight-track audio tape player and the burgeoning of cell phones demonstrate, superior products can overcome even substantial market entry barriers. Technologies can also become ambidextrous, able to work through interfacing with several competing standards. Structural rigidities are exactly what globalization is designed to skirt, so it is unlikely that the benefits of being an early arriver are dominant in globalization's landscape.

America's hegemony could also be sustained because it could prove true that unique properties of the United States give it enduring advantages. Many states excel at aspects of globalization; none yet combine the economic, political, and cultural dynamism that has catapulted the United States to the top of the international order. Hong Kong has a more open and vibrant economy; the Scandinavian countries have more transparent and representative democracies; Russia, China, Brazil, and India have advantages of scale beyond what the United States can amass; most of the developed world has superior infrastructure and takes more generous care of society's unfortunates. What America has is a belief in the individual, and our greatness emanates from this. We are a society

2. Barbara Hamby, "Ode to American English," in *Babel* (Pittsburgh, PA: University of Pittsburgh Press, 2004).

constructed to give individuals opportunity, a philosophy that courses through our political system, our economy, our schools. It is our defining cultural myth. The American dream remains the iconography of our success, surprisingly resilient and surprisingly difficult for others to imitate in its many facets.

This chapter briefly outlines the major elements of globalization and assesses how globalization is affecting the international order. Its central occupations are explaining why the United States has been so stampedingly successful in this round of globalization and exploring whether that hegemony is sustainable. It concludes that those fearful of American power expanding with globalization are very likely right: the empowerment of the individual that globalization is fostering, the fundamental compatibility of American culture with that empowerment, and the difficulties other states experience in loosening control are likely to keep the United States dominant in the international order for a very long time.

The Major Elements of Globalization

The term globalization describes the phenomena of increased activity beyond state borders, principally in the areas of information and economic activity. To globalize is to use the flow of information, capital, labor, and goods to surmount the barriers of localized demand, distance, market size, labor productivity, and protectionism. That is, globalization represents a technologically enabled leap-frog over local barriers to a more efficient market. It is the free market on a global scale, made possible by dramatic improvements in the speed by which accurate information and money can be transmitted and goods can be transported.[3]

Capital markets appear to be the sector most affected by the accessibility of information and by the technologically enabled speed of action in this round of globalization. In fact, Kenneth Waltz argues persuasively that the economy is not experiencing a wholesale globalization; the effervescence of capital markets is creating a misperception that other sectors will follow.[4] This seems counterintuitive given the availability

3. *Globalization: Threat or Opportunity,* International Monetary Fund, Issue Brief, April 12, 2000, http://www.imf.org/external/np/exr/ib/2000/041200.htm#II.
4. Kenneth Waltz, *Globalization and Governance,* American Political Science Association, PS online, December 1999.

of imported fresh fruit out of season, the ferocity with which governments are protecting inefficient but culturally treasured pockets of national production, the outsourcing of manufacturing, and the frequency
of international travel. It does, however, seem true that globalization is
producing at least a near-term polarization in both attitudes and wealth:
the huge horizon of globalization generates a greater desire to preserve
the local, and the most successful entrepreneurs are dramatically expanding income disparity by driving up the ceiling. Not, it should be noted,
by driving down the floor: the poor are not getting poorer because of
globalization. But the rich are getting richer, and thus even as the poor
grow less so, the income divide expands.

While anti-globalization activists impute a normative value to the
activity—namely, that it is ruining traditional cultures or increasing child
pornography or making democratic politics untenable—globalization
is merely one more phase in expanding the neutral efficiency of markets. Portuguese navigators and Italian bankers of the fifteenth century,
Dutch and British traders of the sixteenth century, the robber barons
of America's industrial revolution, and religious missionaries throughout the ages would not have known the term globalization, but they
were the globalizers of their day. They made possible earlier dramatic
expansions of market forces in the world by dreaming up innovative
ideas; harnessing new technologies; and risking their wealth and often
well-being to test their fortunes, with the military and financial power
of states often assisting their endeavors, fostering tidal waves of cultural
change. Globalization as we know it is not different in kind from the
dramatic market expansion of earlier eras. At most, our globalization
is different in magnitude from earlier advances in freeing markets from
local constraints.

Globalization and the International Order

Academic literature about globalization evinces a fascination with the
demise of the state. Most scholarly commentary on the effects of globalization considers these effects detrimental to state power: states will
lose their ability to control information, to foster economic activity,
and to exercise a monopoly on violence. The most utopian commentators believe states will wither, supplanted by nongovernmental organi-

zations' advancing virtuous policies or global corporations' advancing themselves.[5] There are three obvious problems with this analysis. First, nongovernmental organizations only have the consent of their supporters, not of entire populations. They are not elected and therefore not accountable in the same way as governments. Second, nongovernmental organizations often have a single-issue focus (the environment for the Sierra Club, treatment of prisoners for Human Rights Watch) that prevents them from aggregating preferences and making trade-offs. Third, states have to consent to pass their responsibilities to nongovernmental organizations.

Many are willing to outsource policy on some issues, as the Ottawa Land Mines Convention showed, but the charter remains with government. Even in a globalized international order, states remain the fundamental building blocks because they combine an accepted level of aggregation (the cohesion of nationalism) with accountability to their populations. To demonstrate the stubborn persistence of states, in 2005, although EU subsidies to farmers are greatly to the benefit of French farmers, those same farmers voted in large numbers against the European Union constitution because they did not trust the EU to preserve their cosseted farms, whereas they were confident of their ability to influence their national government.

State functions remain most pronounced in the areas of security, both foreign and domestic. Only where states either cannot, or have chosen not to, exercise their responsibilities have non-state groups prospered as alternatives—just as many churches, guilds, and societies like the Masonic Order have throughout the ages. It merits mention that non-state actors have then performed the functions of states (disaster relief, reconstruction, food distribution, medical care) in those instances. There is no emerging substitute for the state regulation of safety internal to societies. The Kosovo precedent of international intervention inside a state to protect a minority from its government may have shifted the standard somewhat by creating the basis for a "responsibility to protect." However, it is a "right" not generally practiced, as the genocide proceeds unabated in the Darfur region of Sudan. The maintenance of law and order internal to societies remains overwhelmingly a state undertaking.

5. Jessica Mathews, "Power Shift," *Foreign Affairs* (January/February 1997).

States are here to stay. Their external functions, however, are likely to change as globalization advances.

One important area in which states are "losing" their control is an area in which they only briefly, historically speaking, have had it: social welfare. The level of responsibility for providing social services, which crested with state-run social welfare in the late twentieth century, is changing. It is generally accepted that the speed and reach of communications technologies is empowering individuals, from the "strategic corporal" fighting wars to Jody Williams launching the International Campaign to Ban Landmines to a single trader able to bankrupt a venerable British financial house. Globalization allows individuals enormous reach and responsibility. The reverse also appears to be true: responsibility is once again shifting downward from governments to businesses to individuals for solving social problems.

In most states it remains the responsibility of governments to provide, or at least ensure, pensions, medical care, and basic subsistence to the least fortunate. However, the inability of governments to address the underfunding of entitlement programs is discrediting both the governments and the programs with the populations they serve. Decades ago large corporations began offering these services as benefits to employees, either in response to pressure from unions or as incentives to keep trained and knowledgeable workers. With greater competition driving faster innovation and more turbulence in economies, even firms that want to ensure their employees' welfare in the future cannot be counted on in the longer term in the way Ford Motors or Pan American Airlines were relied on (wrongly, in both cases) by their employees. Accountability for the quality of medical care, pensions, and other social welfare benefits appears to be passing further down the scale from governments to corporations to individuals. Globalization is thus both empowering individuals and once again settling upon them responsibilities most societies would prefer to have governments or businesses under obligation for.

Quite possibly the most perceptive analysis of how the international order has been changing dates from the mid-1990s, Richard Rosecrance's "Rise of the Virtual State," argued that the traditional elements of state power shifted with a country's level of development from controlling territory that produced commodities, to controlling trade that created wealth from manufactured goods, to enabling virtual corporations focused on product design, marketing, and financing.[6] States with the highest level of development would compete for intellectual capital, a factor of production that cannot be compelled by force but must be attracted by opportunity and incentive. Competition among states with the greatest wealth and power in the international order will no longer be for territory or productive capacity, but for creative, educated, and motivated people.

A decade later, Rosecrance's assessment looks even more true. His description of China as "an attractive place to produce manufactured goods, but only those designed, marketed, and financed by other countries" reflects the second thoughts of many investors in China. Rosecrance said of Russia, "the Russians are still prisoners of territorial fetishism. Their commercial laws do not yet permit the delicate and sophisticated arrangements . . . Russia's mafiosi are too entwined with the country's government and legal system." For those reasons, he judges, Russia will not be attractive to entrepreneurs, and therefore cannot remain competitive with more innovative economies. Russia's aggressive use of energy as blackmail in recent years and receding foreign investment outside the energy sector bear out Rosecrance's evaluation as concerns rise about the political application of law.

Rosecrance's argument is neither deterministic nor racist: he describes the current state of economies but recognizes their susceptibility to change as a result of development level, human potential, and governmental choice. His advice to the developing world is that "investing in human capital, nations can substitute for trying to foresee the vagueries of the commodities markets and avoid the constant threat of overproduction." They could perhaps accelerate their development by a comparative advantage in human capital, choosing their economic path rather than allowing their territory or commodity endowments to determine their course.

To put it slightly differently than Rosecrance did, the best strategy for states in a globalizing order would be providing opportunity for individuals. Governments should offer a hopeful prospect that talent and determination will be rewarded. Governments could build transparent

6. Richard Rosecrance, "The Rise of the Virtual State," *Foreign Affairs* (July/August 1996).

legal and political frameworks to regulate activity, creating societies that reward innovation and are a magnet to talented immigrants. It is so much easier said than done, however.

The Measures of American Power

The extent of American dominance in this time of globalization is much commented on but infrequently illustrated. The most often-used descriptors are gross domestic product (GDP) and defense spending. These come nowhere near capturing the breadth of affect or diversity of means by which the expansion of global communications, trade, and activity is dominated by the United States. The appendix at the back of this book, "Measures of State Power," attempts to give greater depth by comparing America with the rest of the world combined, along with the United Kingdom, Japan, China, India, Russia, Germany, France, and Iran. The nations for comparison were selected to represent the wealthiest countries, the two most dynamic rising powers, a former superpower, and one country, Iran, that is seeking to prosper while restricting the influence of globalization.

The basic data is unsurprising: the United States comprises 28 percent of the global economy, shifted further away from agriculture and manufacturing than most; is the second largest attractor of capital; and sends large amounts of money privately out of the country through remittances. The U.S. dollar constitutes about half of global currency reserves (this figure probably understates actual holdings; the *Economist* assesses the dollar at 65 percent of the global total).[7] American capital markets attract less investment than Britain's, but substantially more than any other country. Interestingly, China's capital markets have not succeeded in becoming home to a significant international presence.

Businesses have a much easier time establishing themselves in the United States than in most competitor countries—it takes only five days to start a business in the United States, compared with forty-eight days in China and a staggering seventy-one days in India. A third of the world's most profitable businesses are based in the United States, more by a wide margin than anywhere else. Corporate tax rates are compa-

7. "Losing Faith in the Greenback," *Economist,* Nov. 29, 2007.

rable, and personal income taxes significantly lower, in the United States than everywhere surveyed except Russia.

Defense spending figures are widely divergent, with the United States constituting nearly half the global total. China is the next largest spender, at one-fifth the U.S. budgeted total, but as a proportion of GDP, China spends only 1.3 percent compared with the United States at 4.0 percent.

Japan tops the global competition in patent applications, a measure of intellectual capital, with nearly 360,000 yearly. The United States ranks second with 203,000; China third with 93,000. Nonresident patents provide a masking variable for trust in a country's legal system: firms must be confident the information required to attain a patent will be protected. Here the United States runs a substantial lead of 183,000 nonresident patent applications, more than double those in Japan or China. Another indicator of intellectual capital is Nobel Prizes, of which more than a third are awarded to Americans. The United States also has the largest number of *Newsweek* top 100 global universities, with forty-four (only Britain even has a double-digit figure), and the largest percentage of foreign students studying here, 23 percent of the global figure, for a total of 572,000. We have, however, only a very small proportion of Americans who choose to study abroad, perhaps boding poorly for future American understanding of the world.

A third of global research and development spending (normalized for purchasing power) is spent in the United States, more than triple the R&D largesse in any other country. The United States publishes more than two hundred thousand scientific and technical journal articles, again nearly a third of the world total, and collects half the global royalty and license fees. China leads the world in trademark applications, however, nearly doubling the U.S. figure, although again with far fewer by nonresidents. America has the largest number of Internet users, but at 69 percent is roughly on par with most highly developed countries. Interestingly, Iran has a higher proportion (11 percent) than either China or India.

Migration figures trend to American advantage: we have a large exposure to immigration, with three immigrants per one thousand people, and more than 25 percent of legal immigrants to the United States have at least a bachelor's degree.

Cultural indices are squishier but also paint a picture of American hegemony. The United States accounts for a third of global movie ticket sales but more than 40 percent of movie revenue (India actually sells more tickets but pulls in only 10 percent of the revenue); six of the top-ten-selling music albums featured American artists, and nine of the top ten albums were produced by American record companies, which speaks to the United States as a global trendsetter but also profiteer. The United States is a huge importer of "heritage goods," that is, other countries' art and cultural artifacts, as is Russia. All other countries surveyed are net exporters.

The United States exports and imports mountains of recorded and audiovisual media, showing not only the strength of its cultural exports but a curiosity usually unsuspected of Americans, suggesting an acquisitiveness for excellence where it exists in other cultures. It could, however, also represent failure to police the lack of intellectual property protections on audiovisual products or a growing dependence on visual effects studios in other countries. The United States breaks even on books imported and exported; Japan, India, Germany, France, and Iran all show a thirst for foreign literature, but none import as many books as does the United States.

The United States, Britain, and India are all net exporters of newspapers and periodicals (probably representing the structural advantage of English in their usage), whereas Japan, China, and Russia are importers. English is, however, not the second language of choice: French holds that honor (or at least did in the last significant study, which was in 1997). More than half of global tourism receipts accrue to the United States, meaning that despite our unpopularity, tourists still flock to the United States (37 percent of all global travelers visit here) and spend money when they visit.

It is possible to draw four conclusions from this avalanche of data. First, that Britain is the real winner of globalization, the country that profits most and makes the shrewdest use of its assets. Second, that the United States persistently accounts for about a quarter of global economic activity. Third, that the United States is the leader or runner up in nearly every metric of power. Fourth, that the breadth and depth of U.S. power in economic, intellectual, social, and cultural terms combine to dominate the international order.

Why the United States Succeeds

American optimism is everywhere noted, usually with a mix of admiration and condescension: who else would be naïve enough to believe that democratic values are universal and to work to foster them in the inhospitable soil of Afghanistan and the Middle East? Cynics ascribe it to inexperience (waving away that the United States has been the guarantor of states in the Middle East since the British and French withdrawal in 1956), willful ignorance (so few Americans live abroad, speak foreign languages, know geography), or happy circumstance (landing between Mexico and Canada as neighbors rather than Russia and Germany, having a service-economy revolution just as the fixed means of production were losing value internationally), all of which are more satisfying for denying the United States agency, as political scientists would say. That is, we deserve no credit for generating or sustaining belief; it is the result of circumstance.

Such explanations denigrate the extent to which the United States deserves to be the hegemon of the international order. Our success is the result of a confluence of choices by individuals and government that spring naturally from our uniquely American political culture. The magnitude of American power in a globalizing international order results from the aggregation of our economic risk tolerance, transparency, and diversity. Moreover, these three sources of our power reinforce each other in the American landscape, increasing the odds they will be self-sustaining.

Risky business. Walter Russell Mead engagingly describes the "financial esprit" of Alexander Hamilton, who among the Founding Fathers best represents the economic perspective that would shape the United States.[8] While the Virginians and other landed gentry sought a pastoral economy, Hamilton ensured usury to good purpose in founding the Bank of New York and establishing, as treasury secretary, a legal framework for free capital markets and permissive bankruptcy laws. Intrinsic to financial esprit is the notion of failure: economic ventures are inher-

8. Walter Russell Mead, *Special Providence: American Foreign Policy and How It Changed the World* (New York: Routledge, 2002).

ently risky, and their failure may result from luck and timing as well as from lack of skill. Therefore, business failure needn't indicate an unworthiness for future credit.

This simple, simple idea reflects much that is great in American society and is the genesis of the innovative powerhouse of the American economy. Because of Hamilton's financial esprit, the penalties for failure are lower here, emboldening commercial ventures and innovators. Chapter 11 bankruptcy laws shield entrepreneurs from creditors while they restructure business as to attempt a return to profitability. Other bankruptcy laws prevent the seizure of personal property, giving enormous incentive for entrepreneurs to start businesses in the United States. Hamilton would delight in knowing there are Silicon Valley venture capitalists that won't lend money to people who haven't already run a failed business, on the argument this tells the lenders the borrowers are too cautious and their judgment is untested.

F. Scott Fitzgerald was memorable but wrong in declaring "there are no second acts in American life."[9] We are a political culture not only tolerant of, but fascinated with, second acts. Many people who came to America probably had nothing to lose elsewhere and sought the latitude to start anonymous and anew here. They invented names and heritages for themselves, like "Count" Harazthy who brought Hungarian grapes to California to found the wine industry. Abraham Lincoln went bankrupt and had his possessions auctioned off as a young man, was voted out of the House of Representatives after a single term, and was defeated for the Senate before running for president. Ulysses Grant was cashiered out of the army after the Mexican War because of his drinking and came back to command the victorious Union armies in the Civil War. Alexander Hamilton was humiliatingly impeached for insider bond trading while treasury secretary in the Washington administration, refused to recant libelous allegations against Aaron Burr, had his extramarital affair publicized by Jefferson's henchmen, and remained a major force in American politics until his death. Richard Nixon clawed his way back from resigning as president to being considered a Great Statesman for the last twenty years of his life. Bill Clinton not only survived impeachment but could probably be reelected president but for the xxiind amend-

9. F. Scott Fitzgerald, *Notes for "The Last Tycoon"* (New York: Charles Scribner's, 1947), p. 163.

ment. Mariano Vallejo was overthrown as commanding general of the Mexican province of California, wrote a magisterial history of the state, and became a U.S. senator. We not only tolerate second acts, we often prefer them to unsullied greatness.

Hamilton's financial esprit taps into another competitive advantage of American society and its economy: adaptability. There is a fundamental acceptance in American political culture that economic enterprise is by nature risky, and therefore unreliable. In 1980, manufacturing constituted 25 percent of the American economy; by 1995, manufacturing constituted only 7 percent, meaning more than 16 million people were put out of work as the American economy adapted.[10] Not just put out of work: had to find a different kind of job, one that didn't use their existing skills.

While not wishing to lessen the difficulty of finding new work or the griefs this enormous shift caused people, the aggregate political disruption was surprisingly small. There is no American parallel to Prime Minister Thatcher's breaking the miners union in the 1980s; one has to go back to President Truman's taking on U.S. Steel during the Korean War, but even then the comparison is imperfect, because Thatcher was using miners as the exemplar of how business in Britain must change. The tenacity is remarkable with which contemporary German, French, and other countries' unions strike—successfully—to hold back the tides of economic change. The contrast to American acceptance demonstrates the different resonance of economic security in those political cultures.

Napoleon famously derided the British as a nation of shopkeepers. Americans are a nation of consumer-mad homeowners. Partly because of the grand space we occupy, Americans tend toward suburbs and houses, making housing the mainstay of the American economy (with thirty-one people per square kilometer, the United States ranks 172nd in the world in population density, in the same neighborhood with Estonia, Kyrgyzstan, Venezuela, and Laos).[11] Explaining the reliably frothy consumer

10. The U.S. population was roughly 250 million; weighting for half the population as adult, and employment of 94 percent of males and 50 percent of females, would place 58.75 million males in the workforce and 31.25 million females. Of that workforce of 90 million, 22.5 million represents the 25 percent of manufacturing, whereas 7 percent of that total comprises about 6.5 million manufacturing workers remaining by 1995.

11. United Nations, World Population Prospects (United Nations, 2004 revision).

market in the United States is more difficult, except to say that heated car seats and breath-freshening lip gloss and cars with ignitions that can be started from inside the house to warm up on cold winter mornings and appliances designed to be thrown away rather than repaired seem somehow as though they belong here. In other societies there is a veneration for traditional ways of doing things. In the United States there is a veneration for new ways of doing things, especially if they involve technological innovation. In *The Innocents Abroad,* Mark Twain captures this sense with his revolted and intemperate tirade against a typical inhabitant of the Azores for "pray[ing] to God to shield him from all blasphemous desire to know more than his father did before him" and therefore consigning himself to wooden ploughs and penury.[12] Twain couldn't get off the picturesque island fast enough.

Transparency. We are a people made great by our distrust of power, skeptical of our own leadership and governance. The fundamental premise of American government is that people have rights and they loan them, in limited ways for specific purposes, to governments. As a result, American society is centered on the individual as the unit of responsibility, harboring distrust of anything, including our own government, that accrues power away from the individual. The responsibility resting on individuals affects issues across the political spectrum, from gun laws (individuals have a right to defend themselves and their property) to retirement planning (the state can't be trusted to keep social security solvent). The pioneer mentality of individuals carving out a living for themselves continues to mark our political culture.

Ensuring individual rights against the structures of power is achieved in many ways, all of which in the first instance depend on transparency. The Securities and Exchange Commission building in Washington, D.C., is adorned with a fantastically appropriate statue of a powerful horse being barely restrained by a strong man, the perfect metaphor for the business of harnessing capital formation. The critics of the American economy often deride it as "casino capitalism," implying that luck rather than skill makes fortunes, as does governmental permissiveness for illicit activity. This is unjust. The United States has one of the most trans-

12. Mark Twain, *The Innocents Abroad* (Harper and Brothers, 1899), 2:40.

parent and least corrupt economies in the world, and the availability of information allows investors to make choices that regulate the market.[13] The legal structure that underpins the surging power of Wall Street fosters the world's largest and most efficient market for capital. The American market has aggressive private watchdog agencies, a crusading press corps, and a system of government that requires the executive to make information public in congressional review.

For example, the Federal Reserve Board is required to publish the minutes of its meetings, which the European Central Bank does not, the result of which is reduced economic variability and greater trust in the solidity of the dollar because private bankers, governments, and economists can substitute information for regulation: the market will correct the errors. The United States also has the most litigious economy; lawsuits serve as an added, if unpredictable, form of regulation here. Legal structures perceived to be impartial are critical to making investments, and U.S. commercial courts are considered free of political intervention.

The requirements for visibility into government and business activity create a very public form of regulation through accountability. As Supreme Court Justice Louis Brandeis said, "publicity is justly commended as a remedy for social and industrial diseases. Sunlight is said to be the best of disinfectants; electric light the most efficient policeman."[14] The most vociferous watchdogs of American power are . . . Americans. The Abu Ghraib prisoner abuse scandal was reported by an American soldier to an American reporter. Americans did not require foreign news media or election monitors to adjudicate the 2000 presidential election; our own newspapers were conducting sample recounts, revealing political intrigue, and ensuring that information was available in abundance. If Americans are often impatient with foreigners' wanting to monitor our activities, it is because we are confident in our domestic oversight. It is difficult to imagine an international body more intrusive or well-informed than the *New York Times* or *Washington Post*. Conspiracy theorists in 2004 conjured up tales of the Bush administration's capturing

13. The 2006 Transparency International Corruption Perceptions Index (www.transparency .org/policy_research/surveys_indices/cpi).

14. Justice Louis Brandeis, *Other People's Money, and How the Bankers Use It* (National Home Library Foundation, 1993), p. 62.

Osama bin Laden but keeping it secret until the eve of the election, yet no one with experience in the American government believes it possible to withhold information of such consequence.

The transparency required between the branches of the American government is also a significant competitive advantage for the United States in a globalizing international order. Our government was founded by men who believed that people can largely prosper without government intervention in their lives, and so the system was structured to require an aggregated consensus before action was possible. Thomas Jefferson's view that "great innovations should not be forced on a slender majority" reflects the ethos.[15] The loud, messy process of building domestic consensus is one important reason Americans feel more comfortable without the imprimatur of international organizations. The structure of American politics usually ensures a robust debate in advance of action and with elections held every two years, the perpetual political campaign provides fast and unavoidable feedback for leaders.

Moreover, the checks and balances in the system make it largely self-correcting. Parliamentary governments may fall, but they are not in continual negotiation in the way a president must be with Congress, even if that Congress is led by the same party. This, again, makes the United States more comfortable acting without the benefit of international organizations, because the natural adversity between Congress and the president provides the legitimation domestically. The United Nations does not provide nearly as effective a threat of sanction against an American president as congressional action does.

American journalists deserve a paean for their irreplaceable role in good governance. Constitutional protections and libel laws with high thresholds for proof of damage make investigative journalism safer here than in many other places, but it is still remarkable how little information the government is able to restrain from becoming public. The porousness of American government to outside influence is partly attributable to the political culture that encourages public accountability through the media.

Nine thousand political appointees who come into office with each

---

15. Thomas Jefferson, letter to John Armstrong, 1808, http://etext.virginia.edu/jefferson/quotations/.

presidential transition also contribute to the permeability.[16] The United States has a permanent government in waiting, potential political appointees that have an interest in staying informed about, and commenting on, government policies. The tidal flow of political appointees keeps fresh ideas perking into the system and keeps pressure on the government to justify policy choices against other ideas being peddled in opinion pieces and news programs. Of course, it also usually takes a full year for a new presidential administration to form, and lots of marginally qualified or unqualified people make their way into positions of authority. We are a government of amateurs, for better and worse.

The trauma of September 11 not surprisingly created more deference by the courts and legislature to the executive branch, but the system has begun to right itself. Congress began clamoring for the oversight it always had but had not exercised, reflecting a reawakened public concern with strong assertions of executive authority. The courts are again chipping away at executive claims of wartime exigency. America is returning to its internally combative self.

Diversity. The great southern historian Shelby Foote characterized American political culture as being defined by "race and space."[17] They are the consuming questions that shape American political reflexes. Diversity is, of course, a much contested issue in American political culture. How much is enough? Are group rights a danger in an individualistic community? Is there a statute of limitations on responsibility for past wrongs? How can we level the playing field without unfairness to the advantaged? Answers vary, are modified, are proposed as law, are hotly debated, and are adjudicated in the courts. The political principles of our creed and the constant conversation about their application are an enormous advantage for the United States in a globalizing world.

The inclusiveness of what constitutes being American enables many different identities to coexist. Americans of Irish descent can honor their heritage and still be patriotic as Irish Americans. In most other places, ancestry, race, and religion enter into the mix of nationality. In America the complexity of identity isn't forced into falsely narrow confines, and

16. The total number of federal government employees is 2.72 million, http://usinfo.state .gov/special/Archive/2005/Feb/07-100913.html.

17. Shelby Foote, quoted in Ken Burns's *Civil War* (Public Broadcasting System, 1992).

thus being American means simply having adopted citizenship; it does not require the negation of other important elements of identity.

Racism certainly exists in the United States, but our diversity makes singling out "others" more difficult. The magnitude of diversity in America also, counterintuitively, makes decision about remedies easier. For example, if children coming into the Los Angeles school district speak 135 different languages, teaching all children in their native languages would be impractical, making multilingual education a question of fairness to non-Spanish speakers as well as a question of whether we serve Spanish-speaking children well by teaching them in their native language.

The breadth of diversity in the United States means that ideas and culture need to appeal beyond cultural boundaries. *My Big Fat Greek Wedding* would not have made money had it appealed only to Greek sensibilities. Instead, it spoke comically and accessibly to the experience of second-generation immigrants, as well as developing many other themes. In order for songs or advertising campaigns or movies to make money, they generally need to cross racial boundaries, so there is an enormous incentive for identifying common themes. One result of America's diversity is that the democratization of culture needed for commercial success in our domestic market is a microcosm of the broader international market. Hollywood is the world entertainment capital because it has identified winning formulas that cross cultural boundaries: car chases and explosions, uplifting dramas, love stories with happy endings, and the occasional motivational history so that the members of the Academy of Motion Pictures can pretend they are voting the Nobel Peace Prize instead of the "best movie" category of the Oscars.

Immigration is the generator of our diversity and the lifeblood—quite literally—of America's constant renewal. Until the 1930s, immigration to the United States was largely restricted to European immigrants, and even in that narrow stripe of differences melding races, religions, and histories proved difficult.[18] But the lure of opportunity gives the United States "the right kind of immigrants," by which is meant hardwork-

18. For a terrific history of the mainstreaming of Irish immigrants in the nineteenth century, in part through the virulence of their racism against blacks, see Noel Ignatiev, *How The Irish Became White* (New York: Routledge, 1995).

ing, willing to assimilate, wanting to have what we have. The reason baseball is such a popular sport in the United States is that its invention and expansion coincided with the great waves of immigration, and new immigrants wanted to adopt a uniquely American game.[19]

An immigrant to Norway (which has not permitted immigration except for family unification or asylum since 1973) has, on average, been denied admission to twelve other countries. By contrast, the United States is usually the port of first resort for immigrants, and especially those immigrants who simply want opportunity. The benefits accorded newly arrived people in the United States are not so attractive as to make it a destination of choice for immigrants that are not hardworking, and therefore we draw immigrants that contribute mightily to our well-being. The American dream is about hard work and opportunity. The ability to land safely in the middle class in a single generation is a powerful magnet to the hardest-working and most capable people facing barriers in other places. As a German commentator on immigration sadly notes, "there is no 'German dream.'"[20]

If globalization is often rendered as Americanization because it has a language and the language is English, globalization also has a face, and it is—alarmingly enough—Arnold Schwarzenegger. Schwarzenegger's story is both uniquely American and totemic of the pulsating power of American society. His excellence as a bodybuilder and his personal magnetism garnered him Hollywood movie opportunities. His canny selection of acting parts (and good luck) created memorable box office characters; his business acumen made him a fortune. He took American citizenship and married into a cachet political family. He capitalized on his celebrity to fuel a loophole political campaign possible only in California, was elected governor of a state of 36 million people with the sixth largest economy in the world, and is considered a model moderate and a power broker for Republican national candidates. The only opportunity closed to him since he is not a native born American, is the presidency (without amendment of the Constitution, which has happened twenty-seven times and is even advocated in this instance by that

19. Bill Veeck, *Veeck as in Wreck* (University of Chicago, 1962).

20. Arnd Hentze (foreign news editor, ARD Television), interview by the author, December 11, 2006.

most affectionate watchdog of America, the *Economist* magazine). It's the American dream, a meteoric rise difficult to imagine anyplace except in the United States.

The experience in more modest dimensions is repeated so often in various forms that both Americans and foreigners believe we remain the land of opportunity. The child of Jamaican immigrants grows up to be the chairman of the Joint Chiefs of Staff, the child of Czech immigrants grows up to be secretary of state, a college dropout founds a behemoth software empire from his parents' garage, the child of parents who can't speak English goes to Harvard. America represents opportunity. In a way that seems affectingly American, we represent ideas that have a compelling magnetism: that economic and social mobility are possible through hard work; that in the space of a single generation, an immigrant can land safely in the middle class; that opportunity and justice are blind to race and class and religion; that diversity need not be fracturing to a society when nationality carries powerful centripetal forces.

Needless to say, these myths are not wholly true. For most Americans, where they end up largely depends on where they began. The cruel cycle of poverty begetting bad schools begetting poor educational opportunities begetting a trapped underclass occurs far too often in America. Many of our least fortunate lose hope, and most of the rest of society has lost interest in their welfare. There are racial and other barriers to advancement for many Americans. Racism is a fact of American life; however, it is also true that we as a society struggle to live up to our creed. We at least passively reject that things should be as they are or remain so—and therein lies the secret to our success. As a society, we have optimism that the future can be made better than the present, that problems get solved, that we can build a better mousetrap.

How important is language? One reason cultural purists resent globalization is that it has a lingua franca: English. Or to be more precise, American. People who buy Microsoft products in the United Kingdom have the option of programming their computer dictionaries in "English" or "British English." International capital markets conduct commerce in English, international scientific fora publish papers in English, international news programming began in English, travelers in foreign countries who cannot speak the local language will resort to English, movies seeking international audiences will be subtitled in English, business school applicants want to be taught in English. Thus, the early lead of American influence on globalization is self-reinforcing—language is a sector with a natural tendency toward monopoly.

English having become the language of globalization is not an American advantage in the same way our political culture of individual responsibility, governmental structure requiring consensus building, continual struggle with race, and attractiveness of opportunity are. That English is the language of globalization seems more a consequence of other factors. If American movies weren't in demand, it wouldn't matter whether they were in English. If doing business in the American market weren't so lucrative, or raising capital on Wall Street or in Silicon Valley so efficient, businesspeople wouldn't speak English. That English is globalization's mother tongue is undoubtedly an advantage, however, especially when it is also spoken by other former British colonies that account for nearly 2 billion of the world's 6.6 billion people.[21]

Rule setting. A final advantage accruing to the United States in the age of globalization is that we are the guarantor of the international order. We set the rules of interaction, and we have set them in a way advantageous to others as well as to ourselves. By setting rules that are generally accorded to be beneficial and fair, the cost of upholding them is relatively low.

The United States and its European allies were the principal architects after World War II of the three parts of an international order:

1. Financial management first through the Bretton Woods Agreements, the International Monetary Fund (IMF), and the World Bank, later through the orchestrated management of financial flows and currency rates in the Group of Seven (G-7).
2. A system of security commitments by the United States to stabilize regional conflicts and build confidence among states less able to defend themselves (the North Atlantic Treaty Organization [NATO]

21. See http://www.census.gov/main/www/popclock.html.

and the Australia–New Zealand–U.S. Pact survive, but the South East Asian Treaty Organization [SEATO] and Central Treaty Organization [CENTO] once rounded out our obligations in the world).

3. An international forum (the United Nations) with universal membership that could add to international peace and security by lashing together the strongest states with a rotating set of lesser powers in a Security Council that could take common action.

This web of institutional arrangements has served the participants exceedingly well. It harnessed the strong to the interests of the weak and legitimized the actions of the strong. It helped the return to strength of states decimated by World War II. It increased the predictability of state behavior and created routines for interaction between them. The genius of the system, however, is that the value of the institutions was not exclusive to established members: excluded or developing states could opt in and also benefit. NATO expanded in several increments to include Germany, southern Europe, and former Warsaw Pact members; the IMF was malleable enough to re-weight voting by donor reserves; the G-7 expanded to include states that the existing members wanted to lure into behaving like the Davos norm of enlightened global capitalism.

The institutional order was possible because the United States underwrote it: we have been the guarantor of its functioning. If we did not guarantee as well as establish it, other states would be more likely to challenge our rules. This is especially true for security. The United States has often been a reluctant ally and frequently an inattentive one; however, we are the ally of choice. Mark Twain said, "It is a worthy thing to fight for one's freedom; it is another sight finer to fight for another man's."[22] The United States is exceptional in its willingness to fight for other people's freedom. It makes us more dependable than other states in alliances. While being the guarantor of the order is an expensive and often aggravating responsibility, it has substantial benefits: countries will often bound the range of their demands on other issues to retain a cooperative relationship with the United States.

Guaranteeing security for America's friends has required a standing military force, and overseas stationing of those forces, to a degree

22. Mark Twain, *The Letters of Mark Twain,* Vol. 4. (1st World Library, Sept. 2001), p. 280.

unthinkable even sixty-five years ago. Before the cold war, the United States demobilized its military forces after wars; hearings on the 1947 National Security Act are replete with concern about a standing military becoming a threat to democracy in America. When Dwight Eisenhower argued before Congress in 1951 for the stationing of U.S. forces in Europe, he considered it a temporary measure until European militaries built up the ability to defend themselves.[23] He would have been astonished at, and disapproved of, 350,000 U.S. service men and women in Europe in the 1970s. However, their presence stabilized fraught security relations—less between the United States and host countries than between host countries and their neighbors—to such a degree that by the 1970s, cost-sharing agreements made it only marginally more expensive to station troops in Europe and Asia than in the United States. Our involvement has taken the prospect of using force out of the equation for traditional enemies. Our dominance ensures outcomes favorable to our interests but also to the interests of others.

The number of commitments and degree of difficulty in credibly maintaining them has driven a remarkable pace of innovation in the American military. The problems are so difficult, the expectations of performance so high, and the professionalism of American military personnel so commendable that they have resulted in a genuine revolution in military practice. During their slide from competence in the 1970s, the Soviet military planned for a "revolution in military affairs," a technologically enabled leap in concepts for fighting that would overcome Western advantages. While it never materialized for the Soviet military, the American military began to experience that revolution in the mid-1990s.

The innovation is helped by an economy of scale in spending and a commitment to channeling funds toward research and development. To give a sense of magnitude, the U.S. defense budget clocks in at $523 billion for the fiscal year 2007. The next sixteen largest defense budgets in the world together add up to less, and that's even before the roughly $10 billion a month the United States spends on operations (the Congress reserves the right to approve a budget separately from the operating

23. General Dwight D. Eisenhower, "Report to the Nation from the Pentagon" (February 2, 1951), Dwight D. Eisenhower Memorial Commission, www.eisenhowermemorial.org/speeches.

funds). As no less a source than Stalin said, "quantity has a quality all its own." The quantity of money poured into defense in the United States allows an economy of scale in technological investments impossible even to collectives of adversaries, and as a result, the United States drives the pace of technology for all militaries. Moreover, the large-scale investments in information and communications give a dominant advantage and spill over into commercial benefits (the most notable cases being development of the internet and global positioning satellites).

This brief chapter on the sources of American power is intended to explain why it is that the United States has come to be in a position of predominance in the international order in this round of globalization. It is a complex phenomenon, fittingly, since power of this extent has not occurred since at least the Roman Empire. American power seems to emanate from a confluence of

- culture that provides opportunity and lightly penalizes failure;
- adaptability to changing economic circumstances;
- individual responsibility;
- a form of government that creates legitimacy through transparency and is largely self-correcting;
- multivariate diversity that draws renewal from immigration;
- entertainment accessible to many cultures;
- willingness to protect others;
- military superiority with a strong technological influence.

It adds up to a dynamism in American political culture that is both unique and self-reinforcing. The rule of Kant's dialectic, that the seeds of demise are contained in the sources of strength, appears not to apply. No obvious contradictions shear away the foundations of American power or make it obviously unsustainable.

We should, however, not discount the insight of so shrewd an operator as Bismarck, who famously said that "God has a special providence for fools, drunks, and the United States of America." With all these factors weighing in the balance, it might yet be that the explanation is that we are lucky. Or we have been lucky.

CHAPTER 3

Sustainability

★　★　★

The conventional wisdom, certainly among those critical of the strategic choices of the Bush administration, is that American power has crested. Having reached the zenith of its incline, it will inevitably decline relative to other states in the international order. The proposition bears examining, for if it is true, there is little reason to concern ourselves with managing American hegemony. There will be no American hegemony to manage. Other powers will surpass the United States, and we will be forced to accommodate ourselves to an order governed by a new hegemon, a collective of states strong enough and cooperative enough internally to impose their will, or market forces beyond the reach of governance. If, however, the argument proves true that American predominance in the international order is more durable, the United States and other states will need to develop strategies for managing American hegemony.

Will Globalization Continue?

Perhaps the first-order question is whether globalization will continue. It could falter over national chauvinism, recidivist trading barriers, natural limits to transportation infrastructure, disruptive wars, or systemic weaknesses, for example, computer hackers making the reliability of Internet transactions suspect or publics boycotting foreign goods. These are extreme and unlikely scenarios. The marginal cost of extending infrastructure, willingness of publics to indefinitely sustain boycotts, and incentives for virtuoso hackers to work for banks to repair networks all argue on the side of continued globalization.

There are moral arguments in favor of globalization, as well: it prevents the tyranny of governments from going unknown, reduces the cost of immigration, demonstrates best practices, encourages the flow of capital to rural areas, makes possible the availability of markets beyond local reach. Even if the face of globalization is slick Wall Street traders making money from the movement of money, the world's poor are among globalization's greatest beneficiaries, because the localized impediments it removes weigh most heavily on them.

It is possible that globalization is being oversold: that it is not a stampeding force of market efficiency spreading across the globe and into an ever wider array of economic sectors as the human genius for enrichment sees opportunities develop. The "tyranny of distance" that military logisticians consider immutable may have its economic counterpart. Globalization may have natural limits beyond which companies cannot make money and the possibility of communication does not spark connection. Not every stone cutter in a remote location can compete with more centrally located alternatives, not every business has Internet applications, not every commodity is exportable, not every colorful local custom will be of international interest. To put the argument more concretely, there are reasons we eat cattle rather than zebra, and those reasons are unlikely to be constrained to cost-effectiveness or availability. Globalization may bump up against such boundaries.

Globalization may also be constrained by cultural and subsequently by political backlash. Popular reaction may choose the narrower prosperity of localization rather than the vacuous expansiveness of "McWorld."[1] Robert Cooper has argued persuasively that "the stubborn persistence of the local" will prevent a wholesale (quite literally) globalization.[2] The most ardent apostle of sensible globalization, Jagdish Baghwati, worries that too little understanding of the different strains of globalization will lead to sweeping restraints.[3] It is likely, however, that the unquestionable advantages of prosperity that opting into the globalized market provides will continue to drive individual choices in ways that reward governments' managing increasing openness, allowing companies to more efficiently collect and distribute capital, making opportunities possible

1. Benjamin Barber, "Jihad vs. McWorld," *The Atlantic Monthly,* March 1992.

2. Robert Cooper, *The Breaking of Nations: Order and Chaos in the Twenty-First Century* (Atlantic Press, 2003).

3. Jagdish Baghwati, *In Defense of Globalization* (New York: Oxford University Press, 2004).

where local constraints formerly restricted initiative, and empowering individuals.

Many opponents of globalization characterize the future as one of economically rapacious lawlessness, in which governments will be powerless to prevent the intrusion of inexpensive goods, unharnessable capital, and unwelcome social influences. This is surely wrong, because states retain the ability to prevent most incursions. Whether for short-term capital investment, long-term structural investment, shipment of goods and services, immigration or emigration of people, states still set the legal framework that makes mutability of their borders possible. Some ravages cannot be halted at national borders—the spread of disease, for example—but even then, responsible states can shield their populations from much risk by investing in early detection and robust public health networks. The dark portents for globalization are unpersuasive. States may not behave responsibly—they may choose the enrichment of opting into the market without an adequate strengthening of their legal systems, economic advantages and cultural practices to preserve those elements of their unique societies they most value—but the point is that states still do have critically important abilities to bound the range of their exposure to globalization.

The Asian currency crisis of 1998 is illustrative: the cascading flight of capital would not have been possible had the states previously enacted laws restraining the rate of capital outflow. To limit the speed or magnitude of outflows would have prevented companies from stampeding to the exits in a panic; of course, it would also have probably produced less foreign investment. States would have seen less enrichment through investment, but they would have gained the ability to shield themselves against the economic landslide experienced when spooked investors made rational choices to sell currencies that appeared to be rapidly losing their value. Globalization was not at fault in the impoverishment of those economies through lost currency value: governments were at fault for inadequately controlling their economy through domestic law. If states exercise responsible governance over their societies, then globalization will not be a marauding force.

The contrasting example of supremely competent management in a globalized economy is the combined public-private orchestration of global financial markets after September 11, 2001. When the World

Trade Towers were attacked, their symbolism was significant. It is likely that Al Qaeda intended (or at least hoped) that besides the first-order effect of killing thousands of people—American and foreign—working in the commercial and financial headquarters of lower Manhattan, the attacks would also have the second-order effect of collapsing the American economy and its associated enterprises. This effect also must have been prominent in the minds of U.S. government officials, because in his comments to the nation on September 20, President Bush encouraged Americans to refute this act of terrorism by "continued participation and confidence in the American economy."[4] It seems a very strange comment, the appeal to go shopping in a time of national trauma, except when seen in the light of the country's leader attempting to forestall a second shoe falling: that of economic panic.

The United States had three enormous advantages going into the crisis without which a full-fledged meltdown of the American economy would have been not only possible but very likely. The first advantage was structural, in the form of regulation of currency and stock trading. The New York Stock Exchange (NYSE) has built-in bands of value monitored so that if the market were to lose more than 5 percent of its value in a single day, trading would be suspended. This gave the government the ability to shut down the market. The NYSE had on a few earlier occasions forced a cessation of trading without damaging market confidence, so there was even precedent on lesser grounds. Also, companies had been recently given incentives by government to introduce redundancy into their information technology systems to avert a mammoth Y2K computer glitch, meaning few businesses operating in Manhattan were solely reliant on the physical plant there—with the critical exception of the people—and could resume operations when the market opened.

The second advantage was personnel, in the form of Alan Greenspan; there is simply no substitute for good judgment in crises, and even before taking any action, the wizened Federal Reserve chairman was a reassurance to markets. The secretary of the treasury would have been the obvious candidate by bureaucratic position, but Paul O'Neill was an uninfluential figure both in the administration and in the financial com-

4. President Bush, address to a joint session of Congress and the American people, September 20, 2001.

munity. By contrast, no less a Washington king-maker than Bob Woodward dubbed Greenspan "the maestro," and his judgment was so widely
acclaimed that Senator McCain suggested in 1999 that when Greenspan
died, he should be stuffed and remain at the Fed's helm (it passes for hu-
mor in the dismal science that several commentators noted his Delphic
statements about the economy would be no more intelligible were he
dead).[5] Greenspan was at a bankers conference in Geneva when the attacks occurred, and his aircraft was the first permitted into U.S. airspace
to rush him back for crisis management.

The third advantage was the global connectedness of the American
economy. Because the dollar is still the reserve currency of choice, governments and businesses around the world had an enormous stake in
preventing precipitous collapse of its value. In slower motion, governments and companies can game depreciation to their specific advantage,
but a sudden collapse of the value of the dollar would hurt all holders.
For governments that hold dollars, a rapidly falling dollar would wipe
out government-sponsored pensions and other social safety programs
that depend on stable value for long-term investments. Because of the
strength and connectedness of the American economy, damage of this
magnitude to the United States could not be inflicted without severe
damage to most states and without creating chaos for businesses. As a
result, they all had vested interests in cooperation.

On September 11, Wall Street was physically shut down by the collapse of the Twin Towers. While Wall Street is the premier financial
market, it is not the only one, and trading could easily have been chan-
neled to London, Hong Kong, and alternative markets for frenzied selling of American shares and currency. While canny traders might have
bet on rapid reconstitution of value, the turbulence alone could have
precipitated real loss. Greenspan orchestrated the closure of the entirety
of global financial markets for four days, a Herculean accomplishment
never before attempted.[6] No significant trading was done in the immediate aftermath of the attacks, buying the precious commodity of time

5. McCain's comment was made during the December 2, 1999, debate among Republican
presidential candidates.

6. It was the longest suspension of the U.S. stock market since the 1933 mandatory bank holi-
day during the Great Depression. Wall Street has closed for a longer duration, nearly four and a
half months, at the outbreak of World War I.

to put in place other elements of a strategy to shield the economy from damage. When the market did reopen, it dropped two thousand points but quickly rebounded to pre-September 11 levels.

Greenspan also persuaded governments and Wall Street firms to back up his assurance to markets that all calls for U.S. dollars would be cleared—that is, promising sufficient liquidity to pay any checks presented. This reassured owners of dollars that they would not be stuck holding them when the market reopened, which shored up value in the short-term. He very quickly built a coalition of governments and major financial actors with common interests in preserving the value of U.S. holdings, even arranging thirty-day currency swap lines with other countries to ensure sufficient liquidity in the U.S. market.[7] The strategy not only bridged the vulnerability of near-term shock; the example of such virtuoso management of a financial crisis very likely increased the attractiveness of the dollar and other investments in the United States over the longer term.

These contrasting examples show the importance of leadership, perhaps increasingly, as the speed and magnitude of effect grow with globalization's advance. Globalization does erode the ability to control some activity, but that loss of control can be managed and compensated for. The American military makes a distinction between command and control that gives a useful conceptual framework for thinking about how governments can manage effectively in a globalized economy. Command is a leadership function; it is the crafting of a vision, motivating others to buy into and work to advance that vision, shaping the understanding of a problem and training people's judgment about how to respond. Control is the staff function of issuing orders, the promulgation and enforcement of rules. Both are essential, but the balance shifts with circumstances. With transformation, which is the military equivalent of economic globalization, leaders need to rely less on control and more on command. Instead of preventing young sailors from sending e-mail messages with revealing details about operations that compromise security or surprise (the number of communications being now so large that effective supervision is impossible), commanders need to train

---

7. Greenspan's own description to the Congress is available at http://www.federalreserve .gov/BOARDDOCS/Testimony/2001/10010920/default.htm.

sailors' judgment about what information they can share. Commanders cannot prevent soldiers making bad choices on patrol in Baghdad, even when those tactical choices have strategic significance. But they can train soldiers' judgment so fewer mistakes are made. The example of the Asian currency crisis shows the continuing value of control: governments should have established a legal framework robust enough to prevent catastrophic consequences. The example of America's prevention of economic harm after September 11 demonstrates the enormous advantage of a commander who can use the available tools with creativity and effectiveness in bringing many elements not under his control into coordination.

Challenges to U.S. Hegemony

If globalization continues, will the United States continue to benefit from it? It could be that the inherent advantages that have accrued to the United States are transitional. Other countries that do not have the many difficulties and drawbacks of the United States could replicate the successful characteristics of America to diminish our comparative advantages. Rising powers could develop new models that succeed even more dramatically than have those of the United States. Anti-American sentiment could foreclose markets to our businesses and decrease the flow of talented immigrants to our nation. American society could calcify, losing its adaptiveness and innovation. The inability of political leaders to address long-term structural weaknesses in the economy could cause it to founder. We could commit international follies of great magnitude that degrade American power, or take on responsibilities beyond our means. All of these scenarios of American decline are possibilities. The challenges can be grouped into three categories: those positing rising competitors that the United States proves unable to match, failure because of intrinsic domestic weaknesses, and imperial overreach.

Rising Powers

China. The contemporary rising powers argument is usually primed for China, although previously in the 1950s the Soviet Union and in the 1980s Japan figured prominently as having the model education system, disciplined society, innovative economy, and flawless government co-ordination we were incapable of. These analyses generally accord rising powers all of the advantages of our own society with few of its messy drawbacks. They assume Chinese mandarins can manage an economy without the transparency necessary for signaling in other economies. They assume the Chinese political system can remain immune to de-mands for workers' rights, rising wages, governmental spending on health, or pensions that freight down growth in other countries. They assume the Chinese can invest in the so-called third world without in-curring the frictions and resentments and political entanglements the United States has. They assume the Chinese have no economic or cul-tural cleavages that politicians will exploit. They assume that states with growing power will impede rather than advance American power, when in fact, the United States' record is pretty good on working out mutually beneficial economic compromises and creating political accommodations and cultural friendships with rising powers, as the postwar examples of Germany and Japan attest to.

While the Chinese economic rise is indeed remarkable, there are quite a large number of problems that could stymie its continued success. Eco-nomically, the Chinese will have the challenge of transition from a deriv-ative to a leading economy—from being a cheap production facility for commodities designed elsewhere to dominating the intellectual capital of consumer economies. There are early signs the Chinese government and businesses understand this, since contracts usually include technol-ogy sharing or joint management that serve to transfer knowledge from foreign investors to Chinese participants. However, the transition is an enormous one that most developing economies have not succeeded at.

The economy of scale that has fueled China's current economic development could easily become a disadvantage as other developing economies mimic China's strategy and provide cheaper labor and better infrastructure over less distance. The average age in China is rising, an actuarial time bomb resulting from the population control measures of the one-child policy since 1979. A nascent green movement may prove an impediment to continued production or use of fossil fuels by firms in China, as could any number of social developments. China's fuel depen-dence will grow stratospherically as poverty gives way to middle class comfort, driving up their (as well as our) cost of continued development. It is by no means clear that the Chinese political system will prove responsive to the concerns of a burgeoning middle class, the social frictions of widening income disparity, and the growing demands for transparency as all of these bring the top-down development model under pressure.

As proved to be the case with the Soviets in the 1950s and the Japanese in the 1980s, the Chinese may not be so perfect a model competitor when forced to confront the problems American society is already managing reasonably well. Will the world adopt the Chinese language, whose slippery elegance is ill-suited to computer keyboards? Will the size of the Chinese population and foreign investment compensate for the xenophobia that prevents immigration of talent? Will the Chinese model of making political repression more palatable with economic prosperity hold? Will domestic repression be tolerated by China's economic and intellectual elites? While there are many reasons to admire China's burgeoning economic success, there are also reasons to caution against projecting the present giddy prosperity in Shanghai and other coastal cities into a Chinese colossus. Western firms may marvel at doing business in China, but few would move their headquarters there or be willing to live under Chinese law without recourse to a foreign passport. China's advantages may prove less enduring than America's, especially as ours have been better tested.

Even if China were to climb to the top rung of the global economic ladder, would it necessarily challenge the United States? International relations models are predicated on a dynamic in which a rising power begins to assert its interests, and those interests are of necessity different than those of the established powers, which leads to war. It is a useful narrative for explaining war; however, it is a poor model for explaining peace. One can trace wars backward in time by this means, but it is very difficult to explain the absence of wars by this route without early recourse to tautology. British and U.S. interests have often been different in the twentieth century, but never have they precipitated war between the two, and similarly on down the line for most countries in the international order most of the time. In fact, U.S. wars in the twentieth century are mostly wars of policing and consolidating the international order. The great exception is the Asian theater of World War II, in which the Japanese conquest of territory for economic advantage can sustain the story line of the United States' attempting to hold down a rising power.

The hallmark of American dominance has been voluntary accession. Countries choose to belong to our alliances, make their currencies convertible by agreed rules, adopt laws that permit foreign investment, make trade deals, send their children to our universities, speak our language. Countries opt in because the rules of that order benefit them, not because we force their accession. It is true that the Axis powers were forced into compliance, but that compliance has been overwhelmingly to their advantage and the best deal on offer. Germany and Japan may have been subjugated in 1945, but on terms far more generous from the United States than other victors would have offered and have been voluntary U.S. allies of an intensely close and affectionate kind for decades. Countries the United States has fought and not subjugated, such as Vietnam, often long for mended relations in order to have the advantages of fuller participation in the prosperity of the American order.

The Chinese mostly appear to be opting into the American order rather than attempting to change the order. The Chinese government does not appear to be seeking to restructure the rules but to compete fiercely within the rules, and as more of those rules protect Chinese businesses in areas such as the enforcement of trade deals and preservation of intellectual property rights, their compliance expands. The $573 billion in American treasuries held by the Chinese government and quasi-government companies—70 percent of their total currency holdings—are often touted as a specter of our vulnerability to Chinese blackmail; however, as the September 11 example highlighted, that influential stake in the American economy likewise gives China exposure should it fail. One would have to go pretty far down the paranoid path to believe Chinese holdings were intended for damage, rather than accept the quotidian explanation of China needing economic safe harbor, and where better than in the world's most productive economy that is also China's largest trading partner? Withholding Chinese currency from open exchange does, as Congress has begun loudly braying, give China an unfair trade advantage, but undervaluing currency is a practice not unknown to the American government, either, and China appears on the path to a convertible yuan. And many of the advisors to the Chinese on these issues are American economists and bankers, further increasing the odds that the Chinese economy will move into the American order and compete by mutually accepted rules that have in the past spurred greater U.S. innovation and productivity.

Another way to gauge whether a rising China is likely to become a challenger for U.S. hegemony is to ask which country has the deepest economic and cultural intertwining with China? The United States is its largest market, its largest investor, and our debt is providing the safe harbor for their money. There are 3.4 million Chinese Americans, the largest group of Asian Americans. Colleges in the United States are also educating seventy-three thousand Chinese students every year—plus an additional twenty-eight thousand Taiwanese.[8] Those students that return to China probably do not hope their teenage children dress like ours or listen to American music, but they very likely do want a society that provides such an expanse of opportunity that their children will live better lives than they have, and a government they can hold accountable the way Americans can.

Even in the security arena, the Chinese may bridle at American pledges to defend Taiwan, but the United States is also the main constraint on Taiwanese behavior. China could even be considered the main beneficiary of American security commitments in the Pacific, as those constrain Japan in ways acceptable to other Asian states and ensure a peaceful status quo in which the Chinese can build their own capabilities before having to defend their interests. There exist many issues on which U.S. and Chinese security interests coincide, and in which the United States will seek to address Chinese concerns and to encourage a prominent Chinese role: handling the North Korean nuclear threat, freedom of navigation in the South China Sea, assisting moderate Islam in Indonesia and other Asian Muslim countries, and ensuring energy distribution. Their strength does not necessarily become our weakness; the handling of such strengths and weaknesses to mutual advantage has been the pattern of American relations with rising powers.

It can even be argued that the United States has a natural affinity for rising powers, or at least pays attention to getting relationships right as potential challengers rise. Culturally, we understand their grasping

8. The figure includes sixty-five thousand mainland Chinese and eight thousand Hong Kong students. See U.S. Department of State, http://usinfo.state.gov/scv/Archive/2005/Jun/15-159636.html.

ambition and arriviste tastes because we share them. Philosophically, we admire the optimism and pluck, and understand the nationalism, that accompanies newfound achievement. Their behavior is comprehensible to us, because it is how we would, and do, behave. What the United States tends to fail to understand is much more often the resentful self-defeatingness of states that believe they deserve to be successful but are not. It is difficult for us to anticipate the behavior of states that will accept failure for themselves in order that a despised other will also fail. The point is illustrated by the Russian joke Americans seldom understand: In a time of famine, there are two Russian farms. One is doing much better than the other because the farmer has a cow to milk. God offers the starving farmer one wish, and he wishes his neighbor's cow would die. Americans, being fortunate, are also optimistic, so we culturally resonate with other successful cultures.

It is therefore not surprising that the countries the United States has had the most positive relationships with in the past few years are successful countries: Britain, Australia, Japan, China, and India. Japan is in the midst of the most interesting strategic repositioning of any country in Asia, attempting to wrest its economy from political party influence and government control, trying to build a domestic dialogue about responsible defense measures and move beyond war guilt, reinterpreting the restrictive defense clauses in its constitution, expanding its military capabilities to better defend itself against North Korea, moving into partnership with Australia to manage Asian security. All of this is encouraged and in many cases enabled because of the friendliest and closest relationship the United States has ever had with Japan.

If a rising China conforms to the pattern of increasing cooperation with the United States, what other countries might prove contenders to diminish American hegemony? Two serious candidates on a thirty-year timeline would be the European Union and India, and for nearly opposite reasons.

The European Union. EU countries have mature and successful economies and a strong social consensus on political and economic and values issues. Taken together, EU countries have a GDP larger than that of the United States, defense spending of $229 billion a year, and military forces that could unquestionably defeat any state other than the United States and any coalition we were not participating in. The EU is often brandished by enthusiasts as a collective counterweight to unchecked U.S. power in the world. In fact, the EU has actually performed as a counterweight to U.S. power in some instances, such as the Israeli-Palestinian problem. European states are often the loudest and most angrily condescending critics of American foreign policies, as Iraq has demonstrated, and therefore could represent an alternative model of engagement unhindered by the unpopularity of U.S. policies. They have common regional interests, such as the peaceful transition of "new" European states after the cold war, that they have managed with sophisticated strategies of integrated political, economic, and military elements. They have a diversity of economic models from which the collective could draw best practices to remedy their sluggish growth rate. Solidarity funds have improved the infrastructure of the EU's poorer members, and Germany's 30 billion euro per year investment in its eastern laender have brought the former German Democratic Republic (GDR) up to the sparkling standard of the Federal Republic of Germany (FRG).

With so much achievement, why, then, has the EU not proved a rising power since the end of the cold war? Why isn't the EU diminishing U.S. power? Euro-enthusiasts would argue that the consolidation of U.S. federal power in the 1780s took a decade, and EU states are midstream in making the political compromises and erecting the structures necessary to unified action. While true, three other factors seem more likely to account for the lack of a rising EU. First is that while EU states cooperate in many areas, even pool sovereignty in some areas to give them the economies of scale for acting together, they remain states with differing interests. Differing responses to the war in Iraq show the extent to which they viewed in different terms the threat, their interests in participating, and the political value of cooperating with the United States. Differing responses to the role of the European Central Bank are a major reason the euro has not supplanted the dollar as a reserve currency. EU states are not unified enough to make a run at U.S. power, and European publics last year sent a warning shot to their leaderships that they do not consider Brussels sufficiently accountable. Both the Dutch and the French rejected the EU constitution, and for reasons that suggest we may have seen the high water mark of institutional collusion in the EU.

Second is that essential to being the hegemon of the order is being the guarantor of security. EU states continue to have superb militaries, but few EU states are willing to fight wars to make other states secure. They will send peacekeepers, but many balk at sending conquerors or enforcers. Partly, this is the long shadow of an agonizing experience with the falling dominos of European alliances pulling the continent into conflagration. Helmut Kohl often defended an ever closer European Union as preventing war among its members, and he meant it. Europeans have worked very hard to create norms and institutions that make war among European states unthinkable, and so it is perhaps not surprising that they consider this possible everywhere. However, defending others' independence is an essential part of a hegemon's job description. Most states want a very high degree of reliability that the enforcer of rules in the international order is actually willing to enforce the rules, which at the end of the day means imposing its will by force. As unpopular as the United States often is for its choices about using force, its willingness to be the guarantor of security formally for twenty-five NATO allies, South Korea, Japan, Australia, and New Zealand, with more conditional offers to scores of other states, is an enormous contribution to its power in the international order.

Third is that Europeans continue to struggle with distinctions of nationality, ethnicity, and religion. The EU constitution drafting in 2003 included a serious proposal to define Europe as a collective of Christian nations, despite having 13 million Muslims living in EU countries.[9] The French refuse hyphenated identity—one cannot be Algerian-French or Italian-French—which leaves the majority dictating to the minority the acceptable terms of self-reference, engendering an unsurprising resentment. It is only in the past five years that a person could "become" German unless they had an ancestor of German extraction, which led to the absurd circumstance that 2.6 million ethnic Turks who had lived two generations in Germany were unable to attain citizenship, but people who had lived generations in the Ukraine could. Even Britain, Denmark, and the Netherlands, the three countries with the most expansive approach to diversity, struggle mightily with immigrants not integrating into their societies. Moreover, the aging of the European populations means their social security systems need to be radically reduced without

9. See http://news.bbc.co.uk/2/hi/europe/6189675.stm.

huge infusions of immigrant labor, which will put further pressure on the problem of nationality. It is not an unsolvable problem, as the peace that the United States and other diverse states have made demonstrates, but it is one of the most intractable issues because it cleaves collective and personal identity.

The lack of unity, unwillingness to guarantee the order, and struggle with identity make the EU an unlikely challenger to American hegemony. Even if unity were achieved, it is unlikely to be attained on the basis of a more broad-shouldered, assertive EU that will police the international order. The heady days of European triumphalism have given way to a lack of confidence by Europeans in their ability to succeed in the emerging order. It is evident in their efforts to preserve an eroding status quo, both economically and politically.

India. The strengths and problems India faces as a rising power are in many ways the inverse of those of the EU: it is a young population (mean age is only 22) with a cadre of relatively inexpensive, well-educated, entrepreneurial, English-speaking professionals that have become a magnet for outsourcing back-office work from developed countries. It manages diversity well and has a buoyant sense of confidence about its prospects in a globalized world. In contrast to China, it is an established democracy with press freedom and nothing to fear from the individual empowerment globalization is fostering.

India's problems are the challenges of squalor. Poverty continues at shocking levels. Many of its most talented scholars and entrepreneurs emigrate to the United States or the UK. While a sliver of Indians are exceedingly well-educated, its literacy rate is only 60 percent, which leaves 44 million Indians out of reach of reading.[10] The government continues to vacillate on throwing off the yoke of socialist or import-substitution policies that have impeded its development. "Ground up" development can only take states so far without an effective central government to provide transportation and communications and energy infrastructure, which India does not yet have. Its lead time for developing into a genuine challenger to U.S. power is much longer.

The United States appears to be managing India's rise shrewdly,

---

10. See http://www.cia.gov/cia/publications/factbook/print/in.html.

emphasizing the countries' commonalities, providing status and opportunity. India appears to be moving out of the "leadership of the non-aligned movement" and into closer partnership with the United States. Even before the nuclear deal, U.S.-India relations had changed in important ways—in fact, the nuclear deal only sanctified relations that had already dramatically improved. Interestingly, more opposition to the nuclear deal came from India than from the United States. Indian nuclear scientists feared scrutiny of their expertise, but political leaders saw common interests in sustainable power, economic compatibilities that made deeper linkages profitable, and an Indian diaspora community in the United States that was gaining political power and seeking to reduce barriers between the countries. As India has grown more successful, it has grown less prickly about its relationship with the United States, and that has permitted beneficial opportunities for both countries. As wild as it seems, in the run-up to the Iraq War, the United States very nearly had a commitment of Indian troops for the invasion. The confluence of forces that prompted the Bharatiya Janata Party (BJP) government to seriously consider fighting with the United States is unlikely to be repeated any time soon, but it says volumes about how much India is changing that the idea was even considered, given how far from traditional Indian international policies such a move would have been.

Summary. The "rising powers as threats" argument undervalues the extent to which the structure of the order benefits rising powers that buy into it in ways benefiting the United States as well as themselves. In this period of globalization, it is almost inconceivable to envision a state becoming prosperous without adopting the American order. That order has generated and survived the recovery of decimated World War II economies, the rise of global competitors, the recklessness of the American political system, and economic shocks of considerable magnitude, and yet it has produced the longest period of sustained growth we have known. A state could become influential by opting out of the norms of the Pax Americana: North Korea and Iran threaten upheaval and gain worried attention by refusing to adopt the accepted rules. But it has impoverished them both and made violent domestic upheaval more likely. States that opt in to the international order are overwhelmingly advantaged. While Francis Fukuyama's end of history is much maligned, he remains right that there is no philosophical competitor to free market democracies. Religious zealotry may pose rewards of a different kind, but no system of political economy can realistically promise to improve on the rewards to the individual.

Domestic Failure

Even if potential challengers prove to be partners that actually strengthen American power in the international order, a second category of challenge to American hegemony is its internal corrosion. International standing being a relative ordering, by this argument, the United States will decline not because other states will grow better, but because we will grow worse.

Surveying the dramatic advantages accruing to the United States that made us predominant among states in the international order at this time, we may well wonder why we aren't further ahead. It gives a different perspective on our shortcomings to invert the question and ask why the United States isn't 50 percent of the global economy rather than 20 percent. Why, with a defense budget larger than the next sixteen states combined, do terrorists believe they can strike crippling blows and insurgents believe they can prevent us achieving our objectives? Why, when most international agreements cannot succeed without U.S. support and participation, are they still undertaken?

An underlying element of answers to all these questions is the supposition that U.S. power is fragile rather than enduring. The economic argument goes that the U.S. economy may be booming because of profits on mergers and acquisitions or the dot-com fad or soaring real estate prices, but it is inherently vulnerable because of the greed of corporate chieftains seeking short-term profitability, huge government debt that will only worsen with the rising cost of medical and elderly care, the corrosive weakness of primary and secondary school education producing workers incapable of becoming informed and creative individuals who will prosper. The social argument goes that American culture is a race to the bottom, producing sexually explicit and violent movies, lurid and vacuous celebrity culture, obese and lazy teenagers wandering

Wal-Mart aisles and incapable of placing Canada on a map, puritanical
religious conservatives circumscribing scientific teaching and research,
suburban suv drivers unconcerned with Americans ruining the planet.

There are elements of truth in all of these caricatures. It seems unlikely we could have ever attained such dominance along so many av-
enues of power were the criticisms actually true, but the caricatures do
illuminate important vulnerabilities and areas for remedial attention if
we are to sustain American power.

Debt. The U.S. government currently owes its creditors $8.2 trillion.[11]
It is a figure so large as to be incomprehensible. It is larger than the an-
nual GDP of every single country on earth except China and the United
States—it is larger than the GDPs of more than 150 of the world's countries combined.[12] It is more than sixteen years of U.S. defense spending at
current levels. We are adding to that debt at a rate of $500 billion a year.
In addition to the sheer size of our indebtedness, most federal spending
is directed to activities that do not increase productivity or create the
basis for future jobs. Debt is a neutral instrument, often advantageous if
invested to create wealth or opportunity, as is the case with mortgages or
college loans. However, debt that is spending for consumption, as much
federal debt now is, does not produce the means to repay the debt from
an improved position.

The profligacy of American spending in response to the September 11 attacks would seem to play into a strategy of collapsing American
power. The few hundred thousand dollar investment in terrorist attacks
precipitated an increase in defense spending of over $661 billion dol-
lars from 2002 through the end of 2005, an encouraging exchange ratio
from an Al Qaeda perspective. Such an avalanche of spending would
only make sense strategically if the president needed to prime a fragile
economy with government spending to sustain confidence after the September 11 attacks. Otherwise, it appears a dramatic overreaction, since
the United States already had the most capable and well-equipped military in the world.

11. David Wellna, *Congress Sets New Debt Limit: $9 Trillion* (National Public Radio) at http://
www.npr.org/templates/story/stiry.php?storyId=5282521.

12. International Monetary Fund worldwide global GDP figures 2005, tabulated by author.

Infrastructure. If places to spend public money were the need after September 11 improving ports, roads, bridges, border enforcement, and other crumbling infrastructure should have been prime candidates. The Bush administration did establish a Department of Homeland Security (DHS) to consolidate the elements of immigration, law enforcement, and coastal patrol that were scattered across the government, and funded the DHS to the tune of $50 billion a year, but little of the spending has gone to physical improvements in infrastructure, and most of that has been focused on airport security. As important an issue as illegal immigration is in American politics, with all its economic, social, and security ramifications, it is alarming that in the five years since September 11 we have not seen a dramatic improvement in border and port security. The federal government has not speedily directed spending, technology, and talent on the problem in the way that would be expected if it were seriously viewed as a defense vulnerability.

Infrastructure improvements are not only important in playing better defense against attacks; the state of our public infrastructure is a competitive disadvantage for the United States economically. Developing ways to screen cargo before it arrives in U.S. ports, using technology to surveil the vastness of the U.S.-Mexican border and to direct other resources to investigate suspicious border activity, designing databases and visa programs that provide information on arriving foreigners and help enforce departures—all are critically important security measures that have economic advantages for speeding the flow of transport and encouraging new applications of emerging technologies.

Education. American primary and secondary schools have been derided throughout most of our history; the introduction of public schools often meant little more than basic education from teachers with little education themselves, and quality has varied widely because funding has varied widely, coming as it does predominantly from local and state property taxes. It may even be mythical that American schools ever had a golden age, since much of the learning was basic and many of the great minds that spurred innovation and prosperity have always come to us as refugees. If there were a golden age of American primary and secondary education, however, its death knell came in 1978 when California's Proposition 13 capped property taxes, setting the stage for similar laws that impoverished schools around the country. Funding is not, of course, the only problem, but the Proposition 13 tax revolt marks the turning point. Our schools produce graduates with an ignorance of the world that does not bode well for our continued prosperity, or our national and international responsibilities. They don't speak foreign languages, and they are poorly trained in mathematics, science, and engineering—many of the basic building blocks for success as globalization advances. As no less a source than Edmund Burke has said, "a great empire and little minds go ill together."[13]

The compensating factor is collegiate education. Since 35 percent of Americans attend college, the weaknesses of primary and secondary education are made up at the cost of more time out of productive labor in the economy.[14] Educational weaknesses are, as they have always been, also made up for through immigration. While the wretched refuse from the teeming shores of other countries continues to become the strength of America, we also get some of the most highly educated and accomplished immigrants. American colleges continue to bring to our country many of the world's most talented students, professors, and researchers. The great drawback of weak primary and secondary education in the United States is that it leaves those students who do not attend college at a larger disadvantage than in other countries. They are the segment of the economy facing greatest competition from foreign labor, and they are least well prepared to compete or pivot to other professions. The ceiling may be higher in the United States, but educational weakness suggests the floor could be lower, too.

Political incapacity. Many of the "declinists" argue that the United States is bumping up against inevitable constraints that will stall its competitiveness. The most prominent of these critics, Paul Kennedy, argues that problems are becoming of a magnitude so monumental that the American political system cannot provide solutions.[15] Congress is too irresponsible to rein in the debt or provide adequate job training or ensure a common language that will keep our society intact.

13. Burke, *Second Speech on Conciliation with America*.
14. Mary Beth Marklein, "Higher Education Stats Stir New Concern in US," *USA Today*, Sept. 6, 2006.
15. Paul Kennedy, *Preparing for the Twenty-first Century* (New York: Random House, 1993).

It seems an odd line of argument that the United States will precipitously become unable to prosper for the very reasons it has until now prospered. Moreover, the argument could easily be applied to the United States in almost any time frame: Congress has always been irresponsible, the government has never provided adequate job training. Kennedy is unpersuasive in explaining why government solutions instead of individual initiative should suddenly become the American ethos. It is unclear why an America that found its way through the Great Depression would be unable to produce leaders of mettle and creativity to solve the problems they confront.

Which is not to deny there are causes for concern: federal and consumer debt, education, a growing entitlement mentality. But why should we believe that present and future generations will be less innovative and adaptable than former? Nobel Prize—winning economist Thomas Schelling has taken this counterargument to its extreme, suggesting that we can entrust the problems of the future, such as global warming, to the ingenuity and self-interest of future generations and should instead focus resources on current injustices, such as poverty.[16]

The final rebuttal to the declinists is that success is a relative and not an absolute quality: we don't need to be perfect, just better than the competition. For all its problems and frictions and shameful failures, the United States is well-postured to retain its dominance of the global order for the foreseeable future. If globalization is eroding state control and forcing responsibility downward to the individual, Americans will hold a significant advantage over most other political cultures because of our reverence for individual rights and openness to individual reward. If globalization places a premium on cross-cultural acceptability, American diversity allows our domestic market to be an incubator for products that will be successful internationally. If state power relies more on a competition for creative and motivated individuals, the American dream will continue to be a magnet for immigrants that perpetuate American hegemony.

16. Thomas Schelling, address to the University of Maryland School of Public Affairs, September 1999.

Imperial Overreach

The last of the critiques of sustained American hegemony also comes from the political theorists of international relations (as had the earlier argument that countries naturally cooperate to diminish a hegemon). It explains the faltering of great empires as a function of their responsibilities outstripping their strength. Athens cannot hold its allies except by murdering entire defecting populations, and sinks to being no better than the Spartan despotism it fights a decade defending itself against; Rome conquers more territory than its legions can defend and is consumed in subduing constant rebellions; Britain establishes an empire on which the sun never sets and goes bankrupt preserving freedom of navigation and suppressing nationalist uprisings in its colonies. The argument basically treats empires as though they cannot prevent themselves taking on more responsibilities, like a person who cannot stop eating and dies of digestive failure. Despite the simile, imperial overstretch is an alluring theory because all empires eventually decline, and all for the same reason, which is their power diminishes. It is, however, not an explanation.

Imperial overreach works better as a retrospective description than a predictive theory. One can discern with hindsight that Rome had extended itself too thinly to preserve its periphery; that Athens was surrendering its moral authority in ways that corroded its leadership of the essential alliance against Sparta; that the British had not adequately created a means of making colonies feel British, even though Britain had ruled them. It would have been a plausible argument in 1950 for excluding Korea from the sphere of U.S. influence, as Dean Acheson notoriously did, possibly prompting the North Korean invasion of South Korea and surely prompting a greater investment by the United States in contesting the invasion than it had been making in preserving the established order before the invasion.

The trick in making imperial overstretch into more than a cautionary byword is being able to see that pattern in real time. The difficulty is rather like the Federal Reserve intervening to deflate stock or housing bubbles: responsible regulators want to allow the creation of value to reach its zenith before reining it in, and acting too early robs wealth from the potential transactions, but you can't tell a bubble is going to burst until it bursts. The regulators' performance can only be graded once you know the bubble has burst. America is an unlikely candidate for demise by this means, because we are in many ways an accidental empire. To be pedantic about it, an empire is only constituted when peoples are forcibly subjected; voluntary collusion is alliance, not the relation between an imperial power and a tributary. So Germany would be part of American empire in 1945, but with the return of German sovereignty in 1954, it ceases to be part of American empire by definition.

Politically, we abjure the label—others talk of the American empire, but Americans neither aspire to the title (as Athens, Rome, and Britain did in their time) nor feel comfortable accepting the mantle. Who we are domestically has made us into a colossus, but at least until September 11, we could still think of ourselves as likable and unexceptional. The American empire is largely voluntary, with others choosing to opt into it. So when the fury of Somalis dragging dead American soldiers through the streets of Mogadishu or Iraqis burning bodies of American civilian contractors occurs, it still surprises us. Romans might have been frightened by reports of those occurrences from the edges of empire, but they wouldn't have been surprised. They held their sway by force, whereas we mostly do not think of ourselves in that way. How we treated Germany and Japan is the subliminal model in the American consciousness of power: impose your will, but on terms that will make your former enemies want to become what you want them to become, and enjoy their partnership in their later peace and prosperity. We expect to be a force for good in the world, and cannot long sustain domestic support for wars without that narrative as justification.

September 11 changed American consciousness of power in a way comparable to Adam and Eve's noticing their nakedness after the apple—we were suddenly aware of how dominant we were in the international order. Before September 11 the reverse seemed almost to be true: far from believing we had the ability to accomplish anything, we more often—as a society, not individual presidential administrations— believed we were no different from other states, no better suited to power, unexceptional as states go. There have been the occasional triumphalist outbursts (Madeleine Albright's crowing about the United States' being "the indispensable nation" comes embarrassingly to mind), but for the most part American perceptions of American power undervalue it to a much greater degree than non-Americans do. We don't believe we have the ability to force a settlement between Israel and Palestine, even if European and Middle Eastern states believe we do.

Americans are also cost conscious, as empires go. We hesitate to become embroiled in many problems, knowing the American people are skeptical of such obligations. More often than not we have to be cajoled into participation, whether by Britain in World War II or America's NATO allies in the Balkan wars of the 1990s. It's ironic, then, that we end up the guarantor of the international order, but if we examine each sequential commitment, the Congress and the public in every instance have required considerable persuasion and time. Committing to the European theater in World War II would have been a hard sell had Hitler not foolishly declared war on us. Dean Acheson publicly ruminated on South Korea's being outside the perimeter of American commitments before North Korea's attack moved the line for the Truman administration. Securing congressional support for NATO commitments was a very hard sell in 1949, and the troop stationing needed for the integrated military command would have been impossible before the Korean War spooked us all about the potential speed of a Soviet conquest of western Europe. However blatantly transparent the fiction, President Clinton had to promise Congress that U.S. forces would not remain in the Balkans longer than 365 days in order to gain their approval for participation, and considerable effort was exerted by NATO allies to prevent the Bush administration's withdrawing U.S. forces.

Secretary of State Condoleezza Rice's judgment that "troops from the 82nd Airborne should not be walking kids to school in the Balkans" captures the hesitance of American imperial ambition. We basically think it's other societies' responsibility to solve their society's problems. This Jacksonian tradition is distrustful of grand ideas and institutions and of our own government. As Walter Russell Mead (who identified the strand in American foreign policy) argues, the Jacksonians are the critical constituency to persuade on issues of war and international commitment.[17] But the United States is often the ally of choice precisely because of our hesitance. It makes us more trustworthy than if we were enthusiastic about the undertaking, which would signal that we

17. Walter Russell Mead, "The Jacksonian Tradition," *National Interest,* no. 58 (Winter 1999/2000).

might be interested in possible gains. Empires look for opportunities to extend their dominion; at least in the twentieth century, that has been a difficult case to make against America.

September 11 dramatically changed this aspect of our American political psyche, at least temporarily. The vulnerability Americans felt after the September 11 attacks may be difficult for non-Americans to appreciate except in light of an understanding that the magnitude of American power wasn't something many Americans actually experienced. As Americans struggled to understand "why they hate us"[18] the breadth of American power in the international order came to the forefront of explanations. Americans stopped to think what it might be like to feel the stampeding pressure of American political, cultural, economic, and military power from outside our national perspective, to be unable to protect a society from influences that disrupt traditional mores and relationships or that accelerate changes beyond the societies' ability to successfully adapt to them. Americans also wanted to regain the lost Eden of invulnerability.

The Bush administration believed that America could not win the war on terror on the defensive but must fix problems where they were developing. To pick up Mead's superb iconography, President Bush shifted gears from the Jacksonian tradition of wary engagement with the international order to a Wilsonian vision of making the world safe for democracy. The first stage of the Bush administration's transformation, immediately after the attacks and culminating in the 2002 National Security Strategy, was intolerance for terrorism and insistence that states be accountable for activity occurring in their territory, only mildly tinctured by advancing human rights, development, and democracy. The second stage, evident by the time of the president's 2003 State of the Union address, was ennobling the work of enforcing our own security in the vision of advancing democracy throughout the world in order to make states more accountable to their own publics and thereby forestall the seething resentments that foster terrorist violence.

Which brings this discussion to Iraq. It is difficult to deny that the theory of imperial overstretch does have some resonance in explaining the choice of the war in Iraq. Even if Iraq was a danger and international

---

18. President Bush used this expression in his September 20, 2001, address to the nation.

sanctions were quickly fraying, imperial hubris rings through the Bush administration's unwillingness to make compromises that would expand international support, shaving back the margin of error in military planning, and the lack of attention to the gritty realities of Iraqi politics and society that would affect the success of the undertaking. That the war could drag on this long; be so costly to America, its allies, and Iraqis; encourage other challenges to American power; and have the potential to fail must quite literally have been inconceivable to the architects of the war. Otherwise, the thorough examination of what might go wrong—the sensitivity analysis, as economists would term it—would have been given more weight. The imperial overstretch narrative of Iraq would see an America grown arrogant in its power, believing itself unquestionably a force for good, unconcerned with others' interests or counsel, incapable of failing to impose its will, launching on a disastrous war that causes the diminution of its international standing and power, and ushering in a new contest for influence among states as the international order realigns to the new reality of the end of American hegemony. It is a compelling story line, especially if one disapproves of the Bush administration's choice of war.

The problem with Iraq as a proof of the imperial overreach theory is that the Iraq War seems to have had only minor effects on American power. Storms rage in European commentary (to be fair, more often in sorrow than in anger) about America's loss of moral standing, and smug satisfaction is evinced by those who would not use force that military force is irrelevant to contemporary security problems, along with schadenfreude that the United States has finally had a comeuppance that will make us less messianic in our attitudes and more multilateral in our behavior. There are even occasional fears expressed about how dangerous the international order will be without American power dominating it.[19]

But American power clearly still does dominate it. The U.S. GDP rose by 4.6 percent a year and sustained its position as the most agile and productive economy in the world. Deficit spending continues, but at slowing rates and with agreement from the democratic Congress and the

19. The most interesting of these is long-time *Suddeutsche Zeitung* columnist Josef Joffe's editorial "If Iraq Falls," *Wall Street Journal,* Aug. 27, 2007).

president that it must stop by 2012. Although they are diversifying their currency portfolios, countries, most notably China, continue to buy American treasury issues, keeping interest rates in the United States low and making deficit spending affordable. Every death of an American soldier, sailor, airman, or Marine is a tragedy, but the country has not been paralyzed from continuing to prosecute the war because of its losses (as many had predicted). Military recruiting is under strain, not surprising given that the operating tempo in the army and Marine Corps is higher than at any time in the twentieth century, but is achieving nearly all its goals and producing the best-trained military we have ever fielded. The military remains the most respected institution in American society. The Chinese probably do not believe they could conquer Taiwan over the efforts of the American military to prevent it, nor does any country or organization believe they could attack the United States with impunity. Countries may descry American folly in Iraq, but they continue to want our help defending their own territories and populations. American movies are bursting profitability records, as are visits to Disneyland and, even with the inconveniences mounting, travel to the United States. By comparison with 2000, all these signs are positive.

In every area except likability, U.S. power has increased rather than decreased. And the likability index is notoriously volatile in the short-term. Those who claim that American moral authority can never recover from the degradation of Guantanamo detentions and the Abu Ghraib prison scandal ought only to review the record on similar claims made at the time of the McCarthy hearings or of the National Guard's enforcement of school desegregation, Eisenhower's denial of U-2 overflights of the Soviet Union in 1958 as Khrushchev paraded captured CIA pilot Gary Powers for TV cameras, Watergate, the Watts riots, or the fall of Saigon. American moral authority has never been as unalloyed as those who bemoan its loss purport. It has always been a struggle, and an unsuccessful one at times, to live up to our aspirations and claims.

Moreover, it is very likely that now, after four difficult years attempting to change the world, the Bush administration is tacking back from grand Wilsonian visions to the smaller aperture of Jacksonian skepticism. Elections in Palestine and Lebanon that brought political parties with direct terrorist links to power, the near-term objective of gaining more regional help for stabilizing Iraq, and slow progress in Afghanistan and Iraq despite enormous international aid have ratcheted back enthusiasm for democracy as the solution to terrorism.

What Iraq has done is to make the maintenance of American hegemony marginally more costly: there will most likely be more challenges the United States must handle, there will be a higher standard of proof required by governments and publics—including our own—to gain support for the use of force, we will need to commit more effort to achieve the outcomes we want. The mistakes of Iraq will make us improve our game, work harder, argue longer and with more effort to understand partners' concerns rather than simply asserting our own, and build more effective strategies with constituent elements that reinforce each other. American hegemony may take more work for a while until confidence in our use of power is reestablished. But the power equation remains largely unaffected.

The imperial hubris argument runs aground because of the self-correcting nature of American political culture. The checks and balances inherent in the political culture and reflected in the political structures of government are returning to form: government is divided, Congress is threatening careful scrutiny of executive action, restraint on spending is returning to prominence in Federal Reserve and Treasury counsel to Congress, cases are wending their way through the courts to provide platforms for limiting executive power. September 11 administered a terrible trauma to American political culture but we appear to be righting ourselves and returning to form. The most important effect of hubris in Iraq may be domestically for the United States, a lesser public willingness to defer to the grand designs of our own leadership.

Does Sustainability Matter?

Globalization requires a spine to be effective; not in the sense of standing up for doing the right thing (although that is often economized on, as Mark Twain said, and would be refreshing), but in the sense of a common backbone for communications, movement of money, enforcement of rules. Someone, some country, has to ensure the backbone of globalization. Most of that spine is currently the projection of an American standard into the global commons. If we do not ensure that continuity, we will be subject to others' choices. It should be no solution to outsource such decisions to international institutions rather than states. International institutions are not neutral benefactors, but collectives of advocates making choices that advantage their nations. It makes no sense to blame the United Nations for failing in Darfur, for we have failed in Darfur and so has every other nation that has not intervened to prevent genocide. The United Nations is merely the place they failed to take action, not the repository of responsibility.

As Americans, we should not deceive ourselves that we can allow other states or international institutions to regulate the international order. Because the United States is such a powerful state and one with a tradition of international activism, if other states fail to act or are incapable of cajoling or imposing solutions, we will eventually be called on to fix problems. Being the hegemon means being the court of last resort. And if we are unwilling to fix problems, they will slow and distort the functioning of the order much as sand in the gears slows and eventually harms the workings of machinery. As we benefit more from a globalized international order, we correspondingly would be disproportionately hindered if the power of globalization became impaired. Our economy would become less able to support the aspirations of our people; our influence and the preferential relationships that result from the exercise of our power would diminish as other states realized we were unwilling to help solve their problems. If, as has been argued here, American hegemony is likely to continue, we have a responsibility to develop a strategy that makes the maintenance of a beneficial international order in our interest possible at a cost we are willing to sustain.

CHAPTER 4

Does Military Force
Still Matter?

★ ★ ★

In the heady days known as the "post–cold war era"—that ten years or so that followed the collapse of the Soviet bloc and preceded the terrorist attacks of September 11—scholars and quite a number of governments began to question the need for war-winning military forces.[1] Soviet forces collapsed, and even in Russian uniforms they are brutal but incapable (in retrospect, the German extravagance in buying Russian compliance to an orderly withdrawal of forces from East Germany looks to have been a bargain). Countries took "peace dividends," reducing their military spending and forces substantially.[2] This includes the United States, which despite retaining all its previous security commitments, made reductions of about 25 percent, cutting half a million soldiers, sailors, airmen, and Marines from the force and about $80 billion a year from its defense budget.[3] American defense spending during the late cold war averaged 4 percent of GDP; in the intervening years before 2001 that was reduced to 3 percent. Most European countries also reduced their defense spending by a percentage point of GDP, but from

1. For a sense of public attitudes, see Charles Krauthammer, "Don't Cash the Peace Dividend," *Time* (March 26, 1990) and "Economic Conversion Crucial to Claiming Peace Dividend" (WorldWatch Institute, July 15, 1990). Powell gained support inside the Pentagon for unpopular force reductions on the argument that unless the military itself established a base force floor, reductions would eventually be larger.

2. The World Bank estimates the global peace dividend from 1985 to 1995 to be between $350 and $720 billion. See *What Happened to the Peace Dividend?* (World Bank, 1996), at http://www.worldbank.org/fandd/english/0397/articles/040397.htm.

3. The U.S. reductions were undertaken in two rounds: the first, General Powell's design of a base force in 1992, and the second, Secretary Aspin's "Bottom-Up Review" in 1996. See Lorna S. Jaffee, *The Base Force* (U.S. Government Printing Office, 2003).

lower baselines the average European defense budget became 1.5 percent, where it has remained.[4]

Among European states without a colonial history, and among many of the other most powerful states in the international order, military forces came to be seen as a luxury good—something to send to where suffering is occurring, to deliver assistance and intervene between warring factions, bringing about a cessation of hostilities and Doing Good Works that redound to the credit of the nation. That the parties to the Balkan conflicts, Hezbollah and Hamas, Al Qaeda, the Somali warlords, and the Rwandans were unwilling to accept those terms has done little to change public attitudes about the purpose of military forces. The consciousness of killing and destruction as a central element of state power began to recede.

America's continuing commitments to states unaffected by the European political thaw, as well as its underlying public attitudes about military force, have left it an outlier among friends.[5] Our role as the guarantor of the international order not only kept the American military focused on the demanding tasks, such as protecting an exposed South Korea or containing both an Iraq and an Iran dangerous to their neighbors, it kept the public cognizant of threats that are not amenable to peaceful resolution or neutral interpositioning of force. The world still looked dangerous to America, even after the cold war. As a political culture, we remain stubbornly insistent that military force is a useful, indeed a central, element of state power.

But the difficulties we are experiencing in Iraq and Afghanistan raise the question of whether military power still matters in protecting and advancing the national interests. We have the best trained, best equipped, most expensive military in the world and have been prevented from achieving our objectives by an insurgency. The exchange ratio of what others commit in order to drive our spending level also raises questions of the cost-effectiveness of our approach to using force. Perhaps warfare has changed and we have not caught up. Perhaps the European critique

4. The most reliable source on defense spending over time is the International Institute for Strategic Studies.

5. For examples of the difference between the United States and allied countries, see Program on International Public Attitudes, *Americans on America's Role in the World After the Iraq War* (April 2003).

is correct, and even for the hegemon of the international order, military force has lost its currency in the globalizing international order. This chapter explores the arguments about whether force continues to be a useful metric of power, what makes the American military so capable, why we have not done better in Iraq, and how to incorporate the use of force into a broader strategy in ways that increase the potential for success.

Warring Caricatures

The realist theory of international relations holds that military force is the ultimate guarantor of a state's freedom of action—the *primus inter pares* of tools available to states, the most important measure of state power. With a dominant military, states can erase the advantages of wealth, social cohesion, great leaders, and democratic structures that other states may enjoy.[6] Threats to use military power influence other states' behavior in ways that advance the interests of the strongest states.

Liberal idealists, the other side of the theoretical coin, believe that military power is not the best way of influencing the behavior of others to get the outcomes one wants.[7] The levers of culture, commerce, government policy, church activism, development of international law, and "legitimacy" are all means of shaping other states' agendas, and with significantly less cost than the use of military force. The use of force jeopardizes economic objectives, especially since "power today is less tangible and less coercive among the advanced democracies."[8] So military force is a wasting asset, becoming less and less relevant to the shape of the international order and constraining the strongest states as much as it enables them. Force sometimes reinforces and sometimes interferes with a state's power, in this analysis.

The problem with the liberal argument is that the advanced democracies are an anomaly of behavior in the international order. We have such similar interests and such an extensive practice of managing disagreement that it is difficult to imagine policy disputes leading to trans-

6. John Mearsheimer, "Great Power Politics in the 21st Century," in *The Tragedy of Great Power Politics* (New York: W. W. Norton & Company, 2001).

7. Joseph Nye, *The Paradox of American Power* (Oxford University Press, USA, 2002).

8. Ibid.

atlantic war. But extrapolating from the American-European relationship to predict the behavior of North Korea or Iran or Venezuela would
be a reckless error. The advanced democracies may decide that military
force is no longer a useful currency of state power, but their enemies
have not decided that. Besides, war may become unimportant among the
advanced democracies, but they continue to be among the most active
participants in violent conflict—they simply don't fight each other.[9]

Academic debates about the use of force frequently get exasperat-
ing to defense experts because clarity of argument seems to trump reason. Theorists from the realist camp often seem willfully ignorant of
the cultural and historical circumstances that frame state choices and
set the price of achieving state objectives. Realists can also make war
sound either deterministic or like a cavalier choice, when the consequences of failure usually make governments more careful. Losing wars
doesn't guarantee an ability to return to the prewar status quo—in fact,
it generally leads to the losing states' being much worse off than before,
which gives a durability to peace and diminishes hope that "soft power"
can achieve the state's objectives. States are often so fearful of the unex-
pected shifting of domestic and international order that occurs in war
that they accept worse outcomes to avoid the war. Of course, states can
make ill-informed or desperate choices; leaders can be irrational or start
wars to shore up their domestic standing or fuel economic recovery or
because they see an opportunity and underestimate the cost of achieving it; events can whip up a fury of nationalist sentiment that leaders
feel bound to act on. The causes of war are as varied as their historical
circumstance.

Theorists from the liberal camp overestimate the usability of soft
power. As Joseph Nye acknowledges, "attraction often has a diffuse
effect, creating general influence rather than producing an easily ob-
servable specific action."[10] To put a sharper point on the criticism, soft
power is an unreliable means by which states can fix their problems. Soft
power includes a broad spectrum of activities by businesses, movie studios, tourists, synagogues, philanthropic foundations to create a brand

9. Zeev Maoz and Bruce Russett, "Normative and Structural Causes of Democratic Peace,
1946–1986," *American Political Science Review* 87(3): pp. 624–638.
10. Joseph Nye, *Soft Power: The Means to Success in World Politics* (New York: Public Affairs,
2002).

of sorts—these activities shape others' understandings of us as a culture and create positive expectations of our behavior based on our values. While military force is under state command, soft power is not in the state's control, and therefore governments cannot compel its application to a problem when needed. Since governments are in the business of controlling activity and want a high degree of reliability that their actions will produce effects, they will prefer means the state can direct. Therefore they default to using military force, the value of currency, access to markets, diplomatic activity, political inducement, and other, more direct, ways of affecting other states.

Another problem with soft power as a substitute for military force is that effective orchestration of the diffuse effects of soft power requires a sophisticated understanding of the society whose behavior you're attempting to affect. Even if the means could be directed, we would need to know which elements in society would benefit, how the action would be perceived, what the choice would do to other stakeholders. Thinking back on the American intervention in Somalia, in which we could rightly have expected public support after the aid effort that began our involvement, is a cautionary tale of the extent to which we can gather and use information sufficient to affect the dynamic in badly fractured societies. It is unlikely the United States is capable of such a high order of understanding, because of the breadth of our security commitments and the fast-developing crises in which we will be called on to intervene. Being the court of last resort for countries fearing the use of force by others makes it impractically difficult to have the reservoir of expertise adequately resourced in advance of every potential conflagration.

In the final analysis, soft power is insufficient to enforce the rules of the international order—it may help create them, and reduce the cost of upholding them, but cannot enforce them. Hard power is essential to preserving a state's independence but often fails to produce the intended effect.

What Is Military Power Good For?

Academics get a franchise to theorize about whether military power is useful because policymakers often use force badly, and often impute to it achievements the use of force is incapable of creating.

Fundamentally, military power can only be relied on to kill people and break things. Military force can prevent attacks by killing the military forces that would conduct them, or by destroying the sites where weapons are developed, stored, or would be launched. Military force can prevent conquest by destroying the invading forces; even if resistance is unsuccessful, the fight will raise the cost of success to the invader. Military force can punish the use of force by others by retaliating with destruction.

These first-order, or direct, effects are critical, of course, even in this age of laudatory squeamishness about inflicting civilian casualties and destroying infrastructure in countries with which we are at war. The threat of killing people and breaking things can often force a cessation of harm, dissuade challengers from choosing force to achieve their objectives, or hold a stalemate in place while political and economic effects occur.

What military force cannot do is bring peace or create sophisticated political dynamics. This bedrock truth is the hardest constraint for political leaders to accept: force is a blunt tool, incapable of being dressed in elaborate designs to send complex signals that political leaders often want to freight its use with. Everything beyond killing people and breaking things that we want military force to achieve is a bank shot, attempting to use force to engender political choices. Force can often buy time for other means to succeed, but it cannot create the success.

Edmund Burke captured the dynamic best: "the use of force alone is but temporary. It may subdue for a moment but it does not remove the necessity of subduing again. And a country is not to be governed that is perpetually to be conquered.[11] It should add poignancy to his insight for Americans that the "country" Edmund Burke was speaking about in 1775 when he argued against a punitive military approach was ours, Britain's rebellious American colonies.

Military force can achieve the first-order effects of destruction and killing. The second-order effects of preferred political outcomes such as capitulation or acceptance of your demands require a more complete strategy with political and economic components. These second-order effects also require acceptance by your enemy.

---

11. Burke, *Second Speech on Conciliation with America*.

How to Use Force Effectively

Force has a limited range of applications, then, if we accept it can only be counted on to deliver blunt messages: we will keep attacking your military until it is unwilling or unable to fight and you are left defenseless; we will kill your population and destroy your cities until you stop doing what we object to; we will avenge any losses you impose on us with equal or more catastrophic losses to you.

Not surprisingly, these are the missions the military is most comfortable performing; they get concerned when political leaders begin frosting the directly achievable with more complicated signals or effects, a discomfort exacerbated by so few political leaders having military experience. While the civilian leaders unquestionably have the authority to make decisions on war and peace, there are often questions among the military whether their civilian masters know what they're doing.

American political leaders tend to overuse military force; they usually believe it is a more reliable means of affecting change than the messier and often slower corralling of international opprobrium, fostering of political change, or alignment of economic policies. This political affinity for the use of force is understandable, since our military tends to win its wars—or at least has not suffered a defeat that left the country prostrate, subjugated to the will of a victorious enemy. So we have not paid the penalty of losing our own freedom for having chosen force. As Walter Russell Mead points out, the weighting toward force in foreign policy also dovetails with our Jacksonian distrust of social engineering and international institutions.[12]

It must also be said, though, that American leaders often use the military to achieve many nonmilitary functions, both at home and abroad, because we lack other means. The disproportionate investment in defense relative to other levers of state power has produced a circumstance in which there are few other options. To give a sense of contrast, America has 1,200,000 soldiers, sailors, airmen, and Marines under arms (both active duty and reserves); we have only 6,000 foreign service officers engaging in diplomatic outreach. In a strict Lanchester equation of attrition, the military has two hundred times the capacity of the State

12. Mead, *The Jacksonian Tradition*.

Department.[13] It is difficult to imagine a genuinely integrated political and military strategy when the State Department lacks the numbers to be present and involved around the world. As General Hugh Shelton, chairman of the Joint Chiefs of Staff, cautioned Congress, "if all you have is a hammer, every problem is a nail."[14]

The use of force is complicated by its stickiness, a prospect often underestimated by political leaders. Once you commit force, you commit the prestige of the state; therefore it is extraordinarily difficult for leaders to disengage from wars, or even small demonstrative uses of force, once begun. Leaders frequently believe they can take initial action, limiting their exposure by limiting their means; this belief often proves false. The Kennedy administration's strategy of flexible response, which sought to introduce graduated escalation to provide signals of limited intent and opportunities for political reconsideration before reaching strategic nuclear weapons use, was built on just such a premise.[15] Adopting the strategy in regional war plans had up to eight divisions of U.S. forces fighting and losing a war in Germany without our government crossing the nuclear threshold—accepting a loss of over a hundred thousand American soldiers without forcing the war to a successful conclusion. The supreme allied commander, Europe, General Lauris Norstad, refused to adopt the approach, saying "in warfare, escalation is likely to be explosive."[16] Warfare is simply not an activity that lends itself to careful calibration in real time, and it is irresponsible to build a strategy based on leaders having that dispassionate restraint or accurate understanding of the judgments an adversary is making while the fighting is going on.

Warfare is also an activity in which success is judged by effectiveness, not efficiency. Operating close to the margin in ways that cut costs is a laudable practice in business; in warfare it is a false economy. Adversaries tend to believe that limited resources show a limited commitment to

13. F. W. Lanchester's 1914 equations are a rough first cut at assessing the outcome of wars based solely on the size of the forces engaged in combat.

14. Hugh Shelton, Chairman of the Joint Chiefs of Staff, quoted in Christian Coryl and John Barry, "Wrap These Guys Up," *Newsweek*, Dec. 8, 2003.

15. Lawrence Freedman, *The Evolution of Nuclear Strategy* (London: St Martin's Press, 1984).

16. Quoted in McGeorge Bundy, memorandum of conversation, October 3, 1961; See also L. Legere and W. Y. Smith, memorandum for General Taylor regarding General Norstad's views, Sep. 28, 1961; Both are included in *Foreign Relations of the United States, Kennedy Administration,* vol. 8, National Security Policy (U.S. Government Printing Office, 1996).

succeeding and are therefore more likely to challenge you or persist in opposition. Moreover, succeeding in warfare depends on so many variables that planners should always want a very wide margin for error.

Containing the civilian leadership's enthusiasm for using military force is a central preoccupation in the Department of Defense (DOD). It was the impetus behind the development in 1983 (in the wake of the Lebanon peacekeeping debacle) of questions the political leadership should address before committing American military forces. These guidelines, later known as the Powell Doctrine, sought to focus the political leadership on whether they were willing to make the political effort and the disciplined choices needed for military force to be effective.[17]

While Powell's emphasis on overwhelming force is the prevailing iconography of the doctrine, it is even more valuable for delineating responsibilities between the civilian leaders and the military. The guidelines make explicit the requirements many political leaders, wanting to believe they can achieve their objectives at only the cost they want to pay, often avoid. They lock the political leadership in to a compact not to expand the war's aims just because the military is succeeding at achieving the original objectives. The guidelines provide an insurance policy for both the civilians and military by making accountability clear for different aspects of the war, and a way to positively bias the likelihood for success by respecting the professionalism and expertise of both the civilian masters and the military professionals.

The guidelines make explicit that it is the president's responsibility to give a clear political objective, supervise its translation into military objectives and plans, ensure the military has the resources it needs to achieve its objectives, engage the American people so they understand what the risks—both of action and inaction—are, and determine that there is a reasonable prospect of carrying their support. The military's responsibility is to develop plans that achieve the president's political objectives, ensure the military objectives are achievable with the force provided, ensure troops are trained and motivated and equipped to carry out the plan, and conduct the war.

In practice, war planning is probably always a negotiation. Resources

---

17. This argument is made more fully in "American Thinking About the Use of Force After the Cold War" (Women in International Security, Occasional Papers #1, May 1997).

may not be commensurate with the need or available at the speed military leaders want to use them; needs may change as the war is fought. Political leaders naturally want low force numbers, believing it will reduce their exposure if the war is unsuccessful, even as they also want low risk of failure; military leaders naturally want large numbers because war planning is an imprecise art. By way of demonstrating how imprecise, when President George H. W. Bush asked the military how many additional forces it would need to shift the paradigm from defending conquered Kuwait's neighbors to ejecting the Iraqi army from Kuwait, U.S. Central Command (CENTCOM) war planners judged 150,000 additional troops were needed. General Powell, chairman of the Joint Chiefs of Staff, added another 100,000 just to be certain.[18] Powell's emphasis on overwhelming force intended to persuade adversaries they had no hope of winning. It also intended to prevent American presidents from losing.

The most important question civilian leaders can ask the military in the course of preparations for war is, "how would you defeat this plan?" The answer you receive will demonstrate the extent to which you should trust the judgment of the military leaders you're dealing with: if they do not think it can be beaten, they aren't thinking carefully enough about the problem or aren't being honest with you. A good military planner would see the many shortcomings of any plan and be able to explain how they can be exploited. If they know the weaknesses, they are likely to know how to protect against their exploitation, as well.

During the Berlin Crisis of 1961, Secretary McNamara's Defense Department developed more than 120 distinct contingency plans for using force. As a professional courtesy to the former president (and surely also in the hope that Eisenhower would not inflict a political wound on the new administration by criticizing their conduct in the crisis), President Kennedy sent the smart young assistant secretary of defense for International Security Policy, Paul Nitze, to brief Eisenhower, who listened patiently for hours. At the end of the briefings he commended their effort, saying that "plans are useless, but planning is everything," because it trained your judgment about the problem.[19] Rather proving Eisen-

18. Bob Woodward, *The Commanders* (New York: Touchstone, 1991), p. 310.

19. Dwight Eisenhower, quoted in memorandum for President Kennedy, August 22, 1961, National Security File, Box 82–83, Germany-Berlin-General, John F. Kennedy Presidential Library.

hower's point, not a single one of the Nitze contingency plans for Berlin envisioned the East Germans building a wall in their own sector and prohibiting civilian departures, the event that ensued.

Clarifying roles and responsibilities between civilian and military leaders has become even more important as we have fewer political leaders with military experience. The great advantages of an all-volunteer military are evident; less obvious but very damaging is the effect that not knowing how to deal with the military has on political leaders. Inexperience with the military tends to take political leaders toward three pitfalls: too great a deference to military budgets, too little deference to military judgment, and use of the military as a venue for statements about social values.

The first pitfall occurs when political leaders inexperienced in defense issues do not risk denying the military all it wants. This plays out principally in spending plans, and most often after a president has taken action that calls his judgment into question: President Clinton's draft history and clumsily attempted Executive Order allowing homosexuals to serve openly in the military almost ensured the sanctity of requested defense spending throughout both his terms, even though substantial cuts were justified by the administration's strategy; President Bush campaigned that he would usher in a transformation of defense that would skip a generation of weapons and put the Defense Department on a sustainable spending plan, but his management of the Iraq War leaves him too weak to instruct the military that their equipment requests are beyond the means of a balanced budget. Contrast this with President Eisenhower, who in 1956, having the advantage of being a war-winning military commander himself, was in the position to arbitrarily set a $54 billion defense budget based on what he thought was good for the economy, and this at the height of the cold war. When Chief of Staff of the Army, General Matthew Ridgway, was preparing to testify to Congress that such constrained spending put the country at risk, Eisenhower told his old friend that his testimony would not change the budget, just the Chief of Staff of the Army. By understanding our military too little, presidents are often more deferential to its resource claims than they should be as commander in chief.

The second pitfall for civilian leaders in dealing with the military is too little deference to the actual expertise of the military. This may seem at first appearance like a Goldilocks counterweight, the first pitfall being too much and the second being too little. But in fact they aim at different echelons: the first is about setting political limits, which is properly the president's purview and about which few military leaders are competent to judge or are accountable to the electorate to undertake; the second is about deferring to judgment the military has but the civilian leadership lacks in recruiting and motivating service people, organizing military activity to produce capable forces, planning military campaigns, and assessing risk. Secretary of State Madeleine Albright's request to General Powell during the Balkans wars that she be allowed to use the military since he wouldn't gives a feel for the derision with which civilians often treat legitimate military concerns about using force effectively.[20]

Both the McNamara and the Rumsfeld Pentagons burst with stories of civilian officials affronting military leaders by asserting that the military's full-time occupation does not produce any judgment unavailable to civilian amateurs. During a Kennedy administration review of the Single Integrated Operations Plan that would govern use of nuclear weapons in a U.S.–Soviet war, a fundamental objection by the Air Force's General Chain was dismissed by one of the McNamara whiz kids by saying "General, I've fought just as many nuclear wars as you have."[21] Secretary Rumsfeld's intense involvement in micromanaging the size and flow of forces for Iraq operations will long be noted with resentment because he disrupted what our military does very well instead of devoting his efforts to issues where the military genuinely needs civilian direction, such as translating the president's political objectives into military objectives.

The third pitfall is using the military as a testbed for achieving social progress. President Clinton's 1993 mooted Executive Order on homosexuals is a textbook example, because it served no practical purpose for the military, but commanded them to lead societal acceptance on a socially divisive issue. The military tends to be more conservative than the rest of our society because the discipline and intrusiveness of military life are less comfortable for more liberal and libertarian personalities, so to command the military to establish practices not yet accepted by other

20. Colin Powell, Address to the 105th National Convention of the Veterans of Foreign Wars of the United States (Cincinnati, Ohio, August 16, 2004).

21. Fred Koplan, *Wizards of Armageddon* (Stanford University Press, 1983), p. 254.

institutions telegraphed to the military that their civilian leadership neither understood nor respected their values.

The boundary on military influence is clear: they have great latitude to shape policies in the making, but once the president makes a decision, service members have only the options of complying or resigning. The military was effectively being told either to accept the president's social agenda or find a new vocation. As a practical matter, the inclusion of homosexuals could be done—having found ways to deal with the complications of sexual attraction between men and women in the force, the military would have figured out something—but they resented the prospect. A chairman of the Joint Chiefs of Staff less able than General Powell would have had large-scale resignations and a very politicized military; even his shrewd work with Congress to ensure legislative relief did not prevent a consequential rift.[22]

In cases where the military has led social progress—integration of blacks in 1950 and integration of women in 1975—there has been an operational need that gave the military a stake in its success. For gender and racial integration, that need has been manpower—during the Korean War and after the Vietnam War the military wanted personnel, and that gave them a vested interest in dealing with the resentments and solving the practical problems the incorporation of blacks and women created. When there is no stake for the military in adopting a different approach, they often feel, and often are, simply not understood by the civilian leaders imposing the change.

In searching for a model defense secretary, one who navigates the passage of deferring to military expertise without ceding his responsibilities for civilian oversight, the apogee is William Perry. He was an accidental secretary, chosen in 1994 only after Congress forced Les Aspin's resignation over Somalia and where several other candidates were disqualified after selection. When he took over as secretary, you could almost feel the building sigh with relief. He ran the Pentagon like a $250 billion a year business: meetings started on time and ended on time, having reached a decision and with guidance for implementation; his priorities were clear and helped subordinates weight the effort of large staffs;

---

22. Eliot Cohen has wittily pointed out that the Bush administration is historically important for reminding our military to dislike Republicans as well as Democrats.

he surrounded himself mostly with calm, competent people; he focused his attention on big issues that only the secretary can affect; he gave authority to subordinates so that more work was done than if he made every decision himself; he held people's respect—both among civilians and the military—by seeking their expertise and treating their contributions with respect. In contrast to the close hold Secretary Rumsfeld kept on planning for Iraq that led to so many unforced errors, during the 1996 Taiwan Straits crisis in which the United States sent two added carrier battle groups to the Straits, risking war with China, Secretary Perry gathered the chiefs and combatant commanders so that he could have the benefit of their individual and collective judgment on the plan and smooth out the problems inherent in complex undertakings. It isn't a mystery formula, but it is too infrequently practiced.

The key to avoiding the pitfalls, and to governing the military well and increasing its potential contribution to sound defense policy, is familiarity with its ways. The members of the American military are, in Les Aspin's words, "a winnable constituency" for any president. They want to like the president. They want to respect the president. They appreciate that the president has a mandate and can make any choices he or she likes about the military, provided Congress will not legislate to the contrary. But a president who has not served in the military lacks the skills they have gained from their extensive service, and by acknowledging that through respect of their professionalism, any president can buy herself or himself wide latitude in dealing with our military.

Introduction to the American Military

More than thirty years after conscription to provide inexpensive manpower for the American armed forces was ended, only 0.8 percent of the American population is serving in our military. It is a great compliment to those 1,506,000 active duty and 973,000 National Guard and reservist troops that the society as a whole entrusts so few with the sacred obligation of protecting us all.[23] It is also a lonely vigil, given how little those of us outside the military know of their lives and their culture.

By any conceivable measure, America is the world's premier military

23. *The Military Balance 2007* (London: International Institute for Strategic Studies), pp. 410–411.

power. Whether the metric is spending, expeditionary capability, weapons technology, innovativeness, or caliber of personnel, the American military stacks up at least as well as any military in the world. Cumulatively, these advantages make it impossible that any country or organization could believe they could fight a conventional or nuclear war and defeat our military. Scholars of military strategy even talk of an "American way of war" that depends heavily on technology and a wide latitude for individual judgment to reduce casualties to both our military and the countries in which we fight.[24]

The Money.　American taxpayers will contribute $476 billion this year to buy an expeditionary military force and its supporting infrastructure. We will spend another $147 billion using that force in Iraq, Afghanistan, and other places.[25] We will spend yet another $50 billion defending our homeland with Coast Guard forces patrolling shoreline waters and immigration guards along the borders, which the "defense budget" does not undertake. We will spend $35 billion on intelligence collection, analysis, and operations that are not contained in the DOD budget. The total cost, then, of America's national security architecture is a whopping $695 billion—$2,317 a year for every person in the country.[26]

Even in the narrower definition of outlays for defense (just the cost of recruiting, training, and equipping the force, not employing it), the United States spends ten times more money than our nearest competitor, has done so consistently for decades, and so has a strong baseline of capability. The defense budgets of the next sixteen countries added together do not equal U.S. spending, and of those countries, eight are NATO allies, and we have close security relationships with an additional five. China is the only country in the top sixteen spenders that is not unequivocally friendly toward the United States.[27]

24. See Max Boot, "The New American Way of War," *Foreign Affairs* (2003).

25. The president's Supplemental Spending Request, "Bush Seeks Billions for More Wars," CNN.com, Oct. 23, 2007.

26. International Institute for Strategic Studies, *The Military Balance* (2008), p. 443. The Center for Defense Information calculates the total significantly higher, at $802.9 billion. http://www.cdi.org/program/document.cfm?DocumentID=3828&from_page=../index.cfm.

27. The sixteen are Canada, France, Germany, Italy, the Netherlands, Spain, Turkey, the United Kingdom, Israel, Saudi Arabia, India, Australia, China, Japan, South Korea, and Brazil. *IISS, Military Balance 2007*, pp. 406–411.

Not only do we spend fulsome amounts, we spend the money pretty well, with about a third going to the people in the force, a third to research and development and to the procurement of equipment, and a full third to training. Most militaries, even those that rely on conscription, are overinvested in the personnel relative to research, weapons, and training. The prestige of the military as an occupation among Americans, and the role it plays as a conveyor belt into the middle class, allow the U.S. military to recruit and, critically, keep talented people at a cost substantially lower than their market value. While the supervision of $500 billion a year is a daunting task, congressional scrutiny, investigative journalism, and high level of professional commitment in the defense community tend to reduce waste, fraud, and abuse.

The Weapons. Our investments in the military have produced a force of technological dominance, the envy of militaries everywhere. Funding for research and development—the seed corn of weapons systems—was $58 billion in 2006, comparable to the entire defense budgets of Britain or China, the nearest challengers in defense spending. Because American universities depend on external research money, and the research problems are intellectually demanding, many of the country's premier scientists and engineers are drawn into defense work. American universities have produced—no kidding, Al Gore—the Internet, heat-ablating coatings that prevent radar signatures (and make microwaveable frozen foods heat evenly), nonlethal weapons such as sticky foam for crowd control with fewer casualties, lightweight armor, and microbial bandages that do not require changing. The economies of scale allow systemic advancement, critically important in areas such as information systems.

The People. The greatest strength of the American military is the talented men and women that are, quite literally, its lifeblood. We have had a volunteer force for more than thirty years, when the shattered sword of the American military—riven with racial tensions, drug abuse, and the humiliation of losing in Vietnam compounded by public disrespect at home—rebuilt itself into a paragon. Our country owes an unrepayable debt of gratitude to those men and women (for the ranks of a volunteer force could not initially have been filled had women continued to be excluded from service) who set high standards and breathed a desire for competence and respect back into the institution in the late 1970s and 1980s.

The renaissance that began in the 1970s was founded on "up or out" promotion policies and relatively short tenures (usually around two years) in jobs to give the upward mobility for talent, the continued broadening and testing of skills, the demanding training with top of the line weapons systems, a ladder of professional education, and enough rest and family support to keep at least a critical mass of the best performers in service. Progressive affirmative action policies, race-neutral standards, and leadership commitment have made the military the least-racist major American institution, a tempting testing ground for social engineering by those who would advance other causes. The fingerprint of its culture is the belief that soldiers do not lose their lives for our country, they give their lives for our country.

Child care, not a subject one tends to associate with the warrior culture of the American military, provides another important perspective on why our military is so successful. When child care was considered a "benefit" given to military families, it was chronically underfunded and served military families poorly. When the military realized in the early 1990s that the combined incidence of an older, and more often a married, force, single parents, and dual-service member families made child care a readiness issue—that is, it affected the ability of military units to conduct their operations and deploy from their home stations—it was addressed with our military's genius for problem solving: child care centers were located near offices so parents could be confident in the care, talented child care professionals were lured with offers of reasonable pay, and care was subsidized to be affordable and provide the flexibility needed by parents working demanding jobs. Military child care has become the industry standard against which private companies are judged.[28]

The military was not solely responsible for the policies that produced this revolution, of course. Many beneficial changes were imposed by the Congress over the military's objections, most notably the 1985 Goldwater-Nichols reforms that incentivized and enforced "jointness" (cooperation among the military services), strengthened the chairman of

---

28. National Women's Law Center report, "Be All That We Can Be: Lessons From the Military For Improving Our Nation's Child Care System" (August 10, 2005), www.nwlc.org.

the Joint Chiefs of Staff to provide the president more coherent military advice, and created a balancing of long-term responsibilities by services for recruiting, training, and equipping the force with near-term responsibilities by unified and specified commanders for the conduct of military operations. The Goldwater-Nichols reforms have been so successful that they are often invoked as the solution to the notoriously fractious interagency policy process.

Perhaps most important, the military remains a learning organization. It probes for its own weaknesses, reviews its own performance, second-guesses its own leaders, embraces innovation to an extent other organizations of government do not. There are obviously also self-serving leaders, trade protectionists, purveyors of false claims and substandard equipment, people who overstep the invisible line of restraint on which the military's wide latitude in policy making is based. In any large organization those people and practices exist. But the ethos of the institution is service, its mission remains so important, and our service men and women's performance of it so valued by the broader society, that it is perhaps the healthiest and most vibrant institution in American life. The American people certainly think so, as the military routinely tops the list of institutions we trust.[29]

Transformation. The culture of learning and innovation that makes our military so special is also evident in something defense experts call transformation. The concept, ironically enough, is Soviet in origin: during the 1970s, Soviet military theoreticians began thinking about a "revolution in military affairs," driven by technology, that would transform warfare.[30] While American generals were writing articles about leadership, Soviet generals were (ostensibly) writing articles about technologies that would leapfrog the West's superiority. Our military-funded research efforts, economy of scale in spending, congressionally imposed cooperation among the military services, veneration for technology, and

---

29. The military is not only the public institution most trusted by Americans, it continues to hold a lead of greater than fifteen points over any other. Gallup Poll on Public Trust, June 2006, http://www.pollingreport.com/institut.htm.

30. Condoleezza Rice, *The Revolution In Military Affairs and the Soviet System* (Stanford: Center for International Security and Arms Control, 1985).

commitment to improvement made the United States military the place where the Soviet revolution in military affairs actually occurred.

In the early 1990s the communications systems that have revolutionized business practices were creating commensurate changes in our military. We began upgrading computer systems to stream information throughout the network, giving commanders much greater awareness of what was occurring on the battlefield and the ability to better coordinate their activity and take advantage of emerging opportunities. At the same time, improvements in guidance systems allowed greater precision in weapons systems operating from greater distances.[31] Technologies were the critical enablers, but they have not constituted the revolution. The marrying of technologies to new ways of organizing and delivering lethal firepower is the real achievement of transformation.

Our military services had been forced by Congress in the mid-1980s to assign every officer attaining the rank of general or admiral to a "joint" job (one requiring exposure to the practices of other services), which produced a military leadership sufficiently knowledgeable to incorporate best practices and work in unison. It used to be the case that military operations were segregated by time or location because they could not work closely together; now they have the knowledge and experience to substitute different ways of accomplishing the objective. They can capitalize on what other services are doing to increase their own comparative advantage. They can compete for missions in ways that spur innovation across and among the services.

The combined effects of technology and human innovation in approach have given the American military the means to precisely apply force across great distances without having to mass forces to the same degree—situational awareness and mobility and precision begin to substitute in some ways for force size.

Transformation, like most revolutions, has been somewhat discredited by its adherents. We starry-eyed theoreticians have overestimated the substitutability of military forces and know too little of the bedrock contributions of the different branches of the military. There is a natural

31. Jacob W. Kipp, "The Revolution in Military Affairs and its Interpreters: Implications and National and International Security Policy" (Ft. Leavenworth, KS: Foreign Military Studies Office, 1995).

waterline of jointness, below which it merely prevents essential learning and the practice of service-specific skills. As is habitual among military establishments, the U.S. military has allowed the standard to rise as its capabilities increase. We also often overestimate how much senior military leaders—who are supposed to be "general" rather than "specific" to their services—actually understand about the orchestration of military power outside their own branches. It did not advance transformation that Secretary Rumsfeld set up a separate office outside the Pentagon, and operated beyond the five-year cycle of the defense planning system, as the place the revolution would occur, rather than forcing every service staff member to mainstream the process. It also did not help that the Joint Forces commander adopted ill-conceived doctrines like "effects based operations" and attempted to impose them on the services and politicized the lessons learned to please the secretary and White House. But transformation continues, largely as a bottom-up development of new applications for technology to the demanding operational problems the American military is facing in Afghanistan and Iraq.

Why don't other militaries adopt the same, obviously advantageous, approach? Even before operations in Iraq showed the differences in how the U.S. military operates, Allied militaries were so concerned about the growing gap that NATO commissioned an entirely new major command (there are only two) devoted to understanding transformation, cascading our advances into other militaries where practicable (meaning, mostly, where affordable), and planning for a divergence in operational practice. But these changes require expensive replacements, not just to individual equipment but to whole suites of equipment. The army's Future Combat System incorporates thirty-four different elements of equipment, supplanting previous ways of doing business. It requires an economy of scale in spending that most militaries cannot afford, even if they had the research and development, training budgets, and innovative militaries to transform.

If We're So Good, Why Don't We Win in Iraq?

The difficulties the United States has experienced in the Iraq War will very likely lead to overheated pronouncements of the demise of American power and give credence to the assertion that military power is increasingly irrelevant to advancing a state's interests. For if a military this dominant over all others cannot win a war against an insurgency, how useful can military force actually be? If America can be tied down in Iraq for years without producing appreciable advances, perhaps military force isn't any more directive than soft power is. If our adversaries can fight us to a standstill without amassing a $481 billion defense establishment, is the investment really paying off for America?

The costs of the Iraq War are weighty and will cast a long shadow over American actions for decades to come. Just as the Vietnam War was the reference point in all discussions of American power in the 1970s, 1980s, and 1990s, Iraq will be the case to support or refute later uses of force.

With the inclusion of the president's 2007 supplemental spending request, the incremental cost to Americans of having undertaken the Iraq War will be more than three thousand young Americans dead, more than twenty thousand young Americans badly injured, and direct costs will be more than $537 billion through only early 2006.[32]

The indirect costs of the Iraq War are likewise enormous. Not having succeeded in Iraq will almost certainly embolden other adversaries, few of whom are likely to share the advanced democracies' inhibitions about the utility of military force. It is also likely to make the United States less willing to undertake ambitious campaigns to shape the international order, so emboldened adversaries will have greater latitude for action. Fighting in Iraq has also demonstrated effective techniques for neutralizing many of the American military's advantages. Other countries will be less inclined to join our coalitions, as they had not anticipated as long and difficult a fight as has been required in Iraq. Without even considering the effects on Iraq or the perturbations its troubles will cause to ripple through the Middle East, not succeeding sooner in the Iraq War has made the international order a more dangerous place.

Learning the right lessons from our failures in Iraq will be critical to avoiding the repetition of these mistakes in future wars. One could work down the list of questions in the Powell Doctrine and identify errors; they occurred on nearly every count, with blame deservedly settling

---

32. A joint Brookings Institution–American Enterprise Institute estimate periodically updates the figure and projects costs through 2015. See http://www.aei.brookings.org/publications/abstract.php?pid=988.

on both the civilian leadership and the military. The preponderance of blame, however, should be apportioned to the civilians, as they set the course and control the process. Moreover, in the execution of plans, the military has done a very good job, so often stepping in to cover the consequences of bad choices or inept execution by civilians that our military is now at risk of being blamed for the failure of the project when they have been the greatest contributor to what success it has had.

There are winnable wars we could have fought against Saddam Hussein's Iraq; the tragedy of this Iraq War is the extent to which our own choices added to our difficulty. The major mistakes that so dramatically increased the difficulty in Iraq are all unforced errors, and they have been mistakes at the strategic and operational level, made predominantly by civilians. The president operated on a management model of choosing strong cabinet secretaries and giving them wide latitude in the conduct of their responsibilities. The conflict between secretaries, weak National Security Council (NSC) enforcement of the interagency process, and frequent evidence of agency failure to follow through on presidential decisions do not seem to have precipitated a reconsideration of this approach during the Bush Administration.

In 2002 the president identified two very demanding political objectives—securing weapons of mass destruction before their use and overthrowing the Saddam Hussein regime—that were new for the American military, without a body of doctrine for how to achieve them or corresponding military plans. Our military's job was to defeat other militaries; regime change required defeating the Iraqi military, but what else it entailed was unclear in military terms. The secretary of defense's principal function is translating the president's political objectives into guidance for military plans. He or she is the person who provides direction that scopes the military planning effort, connecting it to achieving the president's political objectives. A litany of hard, practical questions need answers to permit sensible military planning, and the answers have resource and risk consequences.

Secretary Rumsfeld treated stabilization missions as a moral hazard that removed responsibility from Iraqi society for its own recovery. Moreover, he seemed to believe the campaign against the Taliban in Afghanistan was the archetype for future conflicts, in which agility of movement would be an operational substitute for force size. He thought that large forces served only to alienate the societies in which we were operating. The secretary's ideological opposition to the military tasks and force numbers essential for achieving the president's political objectives is perhaps the most fundamental mistake of the Iraq War, the principal error on which later mistakes merely compounded the interest.

Secretary Rumsfeld's frequent assertions of his exclusive prerogatives in the chain of command—and the president and chief of staff and national security advisor's acceptance of the narrowing of scope for the review of military plans and DOD activities—excluded a wide range of potential contributors and prevented others' correcting his mistakes. Focusing the military plan on rapidly destroying organized military units without entering major population centers does not appear to have been cross-referenced against the political signal sent when most of the population never see American forces; the diplomats and politicos outside the chain of command would have contributed that kind of advice. By skipping Iraq's cities and racing to Baghdad, we left insurgents time to organize their activities, intimidate the population, and set a negative political dynamic in motion.

It would be proper to ask where the military leaders were while all these mistakes were being made. They, too, have a responsibility, both to their commander in chief and to the American people in this regard. Why did no leaders throw their stars on the table and refuse, and then alert the media and Congress? The answer is a complicated but important one, weaving virtuous and villainous strands together: the military's proper subordination to civilian masters, the oppressive command climate Secretary Rumsfeld had established, and a few critically placed weak military leaders.

Many military leaders tried to alert their civilian counterparts and superiors, both executive and congressional, of the substantial risk inherent in the approach taken by the Iraq War plan. The chief of staff of the army argued, both inside the administration and hesitantly to the Congress, for revisions to the tasks and forces, right up until operations began. Military leaders involved in the planning continued to push back against force limits and civilian tinkering with force flows—the eventual release of the initial plans for Iraq and the plan as it was executed will validate their significant contribution.

But our system of civilian control of the military argues strongly

against overt challenges by the military of elected civilian leaders' prerogatives to choose the terms of the conflict and its resourcing. Finally,
the political leadership has the right to choose the level of forces they
commit to wars, and it's a mark of our military's professionalism that
there weren't resignations, that instead military leaders threw their effort
into making the plan work and doing their best for the country (it would
take another three years before military leaders grew so frustrated with
Secretary Rumsfeld's persistence in error that they publicly called for
his resignation). Another mark of our military's professionalism is that
the place where the most ferocious debate has occurred about whether
senior military leaders have been derelict in their duty is in our military's
own ranks. But a system in which military leaders have to resign to affect
the war-planning process—the area of their greatest expertise—cuts out
the most committed people from the process when you most need them.
The system is designed to be more malleable to the military's concerns
than it proved in this instance.

The administration treated the military's concerns like political opposition rather than loyal assistance. General Shinseki was ostracized for
his answer to congressional questioning on his judgment for the force
needed to stabilize Iraq. Instead of being pulled in to review the plan
and suggest improvements, he was publicly refuted by Deputy Secretary
Wolfowitz. The result, of course, was to silence internal critics at the
time their expertise would have been most valuable.

Courts-martial always consider the "command climate" in sentenc-
ing. It is the environment in which events occurred, what people believed was acceptable based on the standards a commander has set and
how those standards direct the work of the unit. Long before the Shinseki testimony, Secretary Rumsfeld had created a command climate in
the Defense Department in which military leaders understood that their
views would not change outcomes, and therefore risked little to shape
policies and choices.

Secretary Rumsfeld's management practices also kept the department off-balance, actually inhibiting an understanding of his priorities.
"Snowflakes," queries directly from the secretary to midlevel DOD staff,
exemplify his management failure. While he would dictate a dozen or
two a day, in a department with twenty-four thousand staff working in
the headquarters building, the notes were received as the most important

tasking of the week, at least. In one instance, Secretary Rumsfeld sent a snowflake to the director for warplans in the Joint Staff that read "why do we need a JSCP?" The Joint Strategic Capabilities Plan is a document used by the military to deconflict competing claims for forces. For example, if there were simultaneous wars in Korea and the Middle East, the JSCP would describe which forces would be assigned to which wars, which commander would have priority on transport, satellite coverage, and other support assets. In asking the question, Secretary Rumsfeld was probably simply seeking an explanation of a complicated staff product; but his abrasive management style and the inability of his subordinates to give any context to his requests led the director for Operational Plans and Joint Force Development (J-7) to spend a couple of weeks developing an elaborate justification for retaining a critical plank in the planning structure, a justification which the secretary irritably brushed away as nonresponsive when they attempted to brief him.

It is incontestable, however, that the magnitude of error in Iraq could not have been possible without complicity by at least some critically placed military leaders. There were validators of the administration's approach whose profession gave them public credence and whose support shielded the administration. One would be the chairman of the Joint Chiefs of Staff, perfectly captured by James Kitfield as "the pliable Richard Myers."[33] General Peter Pace and Admiral Edmund Giambastiani also gave advice that calls their military judgment into question. However, the military leader most deserving of excoriation is General Tommy Franks. He developed the plan without forces for stabilization; he kept the 4th infantry division bottled up in the Mediterranean hoping the Turkish government would permit the use of its territory long after the division should have been redirected; he consented in the reduction of forces flowing into the theater during operations; he reassured the president that problems would be solved and then never directed activity to do so. It is genuinely mystifying that he has not had to answer for the magnitude of his mistakes.

The unpleasant truth is that civilian leaders get the military leadership they deserve. If you respect military leaders' expertise and harness their efforts, they will reward you by sharing military judgment that

33. James Kitfield, *War and Destiny* (Dulles, VA: Potomac Books, Inc., 2004), p. 28.

will shield you from using force badly. If they believe you will penalize their honest evaluation of mistakes, they stop telling you where you are making mistakes. Secretary Rumsfeld's management of the department and the president's endorsement of that management led our military to opt out of providing its judgment on the operational and strategic levels. Military leaders at those levels are already concerned about preserving the force for the next war. The irony of Secretary Rumsfeld's management of the Defense Department is to have confirmed—at very high cost—the validity of the Powell Doctrine.

To answer the initial question of this section, the reason that the American military hasn't yet won in Iraq is that the task was inherently extremely challenging and the administration made it even more so by badly translating the president's political objectives into military objectives, by circumscribing the military's ability to plan and resource the missions, and then by failing to produce the political, social, and economic effects on which success depended. Iraq will be remembered as a military failure because we sent 150,000 soldiers and Marines there, but the military elements were by far the most effective uses of U.S. power in Iraq—the failure was largely in the civilian management of the war.[34]

How Much Is Enough?

If the lessons of Iraq cause American leaders to be more selective in determining when military force can accomplish our national objectives, it stands to reason we will probably fight fewer wars than currently projected. The driver of force-breakingly high operations tempo in the army and Marine Corps now is the demand of resourcing ground operations in Iraq and Afghanistan. Those two simultaneous operations require about 175,000 soldiers and Marines deployed to the war zones. One would think deploying less than a tenth of the total number of people serving in the American military would not place an insurmountable burden on the women and men in our military, but subtracting out air

34. Accurate and detailed accounts of the civilian planning failures can be found in Bob Woodward, *Plan of Attack* (New York: Simon & Schuster, 2004), and Thomas Ricks, *Fiasco* (New York: The Penguin Press, 2006). The best account of the military side is contained in Kitfield's *War and Destiny* (Dulles, VA: Potomac Books, 2004).

force and navy personnel (who, while making important contributions, are not carrying the main burden of the wars in Afghanistan and Iraq—operating tempos in the navy and air force are not in the red zone), and units that do not deploy because their function is training troops or running weapons-proving grounds or experimenting with new doctrine and equipment, the current wars have soldiers and Marines in operational units deploying every other year and reservists and National Guardsmen pulled from being a strategic reserve into part of the regular rotation cycle. It dramatically understates the case to suggest this is hard on families and creates challenges for keeping talented people in the force. For this reason, the president agreed to increase the size of both the army and Marine Corps in 2008, and presidential aspirants are all committing to even more substantial increases.

The grudging response in the ranks to the president's policy change shows one of the real difficulties of sensible defense planning, which is that you cannot build a military force when you need it. The soldiers and Marines being added will not reduce near-term strain in the force. In the American military, which gives more space for initiative and pushes decision-making authority down to lower levels than in most militaries, the timeline is roughly ten years to give people the experience that makes them competent sergeants and captains, twenty to make them competent sergeants major and colonels. Combat experience obviously accelerates that judgment, but not necessarily for the organizational skills needed at higher ranks. Moreover, technology-intensive skill sets are found in a greater proportion of our ranks than in those of most militaries. The long time lag to real proficiency makes defense planners conservative, because the resources cannot be brought to hand fast enough to affect problems as they arise.

Congress mandates that every four years the president produce a study outlining its defense strategy, explaining the translation from money to forces and equipment, and justifying the size of the budget request. This Quadrennial Defense Review (QDR) is extremely important, because it provides public accountability for how the DOD plans to spend its money. Congress can then measure every year's budget against what the administration said it planned to do, and force the administration to explain any divergences. While Congress rarely deviates more than 5 percent from the president's request in the funding appropriated for defense, it often commits the money in different ways than requested. The QDR is valuable to the administration, as well, both to train the new political appointees (the top six echelons of jobs are all political appointees in the DOD) and to determine whether the current course adequately hedges against the development of new threats. It is the vehicle by which each successive administration decides what its spending limit will be and how much capability is enough for the national need.

The 2006 QDR is surreal in its disconnect between stated objectives and forces: it envisions increasing demands in force-intensive mission areas such as waging two nearly simultaneous conventional campaigns "with the aim of regime change in one of the campaigns," conducting large-scale counterinsurgency operations, and continued interaction with partners to reassure them and build their capabilities, but no projected increase in the force.[35] Moreover, despite continued rhetorical emphasis on transformation, it identifies no areas in which new technologies and corresponding operational concepts allow the discontinuation of previous efforts. The study never connects the "new warfare" with the largely unchanged program of weapons procurement, even though the president made clear from the beginning of the administration that transformation required skipping a generation of weapons systems.[36]

The president's fiscal year 2008 budget proposes spending $481.4 billion on defense, an 11 percent increase over last year's budget. Even by the narrow interpretation of defense spending (excluding non-DOD intelligence, Coast Guard, etc.), it constitutes more than half of all discretionary federal spending. The administration has more than doubled the baseline defense budget during its tenure. The amount is so staggering that conspiracy theorists must believe the president secretly has a Keynesian economic policy, with defense as the only area of his social agenda that can abide such enormous federal outlays.

The magnitude of the increase in defense spending is difficult to justify. Did we really need a military twice as expensive as the one we had in 2000 to protect our interests? Is the world twice as dangerous today?

35. See *The Long-Term Implications of Current Defense Plans and Alternatives* (Congressional Budget Office, January 2006) and Carl Conetta, "QDR 2006: Do the Forces Match the Missions?" (Project on Defense Alternatives Briefing Memo #36, February 10, 2006).

36. President George W. Bush, "A Period of Consequences," (The Citadel, South Carolina, Sept. 23, 1999).

Are our adversaries so much smarter than we are that they can remain competitive for about 1 percent of what we are spending? Aren't we overcompensating for the nature of the threat? While the age of terrorism produces new threats, countering them predominantly requires gathering and using knowledge, with relatively few demands for more personnel or different equipment beyond what is already contained in our force. The global reach of American military power that existed before September 11 seemed a fair match for extant and emerging threats.

Secretary Rumsfeld often stated that terrorism poses the gravest danger the United States has experienced. This is certainly untrue. Even a coordinated terrorist attack using nuclear weapons in American cities is not comparable to the threat of Soviet strategic nuclear forces in the 1960s. Buying into a conceptualization of the current challenges as the most demanding justifies higher spending than should be needed to manage these threats. It can also be used to cover poor management of the Defense Department.

Such an enormous increase in defense spending most likely sends a damaging signal that we don't understand the nature of the threats we are facing and are simply throwing money at the problem. It may even suggest we are vulnerable to a strategy whereby adversaries conduct attacks to provoke an overreaction in spending to weaken us.

It certainly conveys that the president's transformation agenda has been derailed, because we are not discontinuing weapons programs or military activities that should have been superseded by new ways of operating. To the extent the DOD is still pursuing military transformation, it is as an additive function, not a substitution: we are buying three next-generation fighter planes, even though we have a substantial dominance in that area and as the missions for manned aircraft narrow substantially. In 1956, President Eisenhower challenged the service chiefs to explain to him why he should spend more than one nickel on anything except nuclear missiles—for all of Secretary Rumsfeld's scathing questioning of briefers, he supervised budgets that made very few important trade-offs between obsolescent weapons to fund more innovative new ones.[37]

What has been done to rebalance spending? The budget slice of the

---

37. The only two important program cancellations during the Bush administration were the army's Comanche helicopter and the army's Crusader artillery system.

four military services has stayed almost constant since 1960—the variance is less than 5 percent. Are the relative weights each service carries in the new security environment really no different? Has competition for mission areas produced no different outcomes? Do technologies or new practices or new demands not justify more substantial departures?

The size of defense spending is perhaps most damaging because it prevents investment in other elements of national security that are badly underresourced. The argument is very strong for spending an added $80 billion to increase the number of intelligence operatives and analysts and diplomats and immigration officers and agriculture specialists and justice system advisors and experts in international finance. It serves the country poorly that we are not forcing trade-offs of that kind and radically increasing our capacity for nonmilitary effects. The State Department has nearly a thousand people in Baghdad, our largest diplomatic post in the world, and yet the number is manifestly too small for the work that needs to be done with a fledgling Iraqi democracy, since the State Department is asking the Defense Department to fill one-third of the posts in the increased civilian commitment to Iraq that the president announced in his 2007 State of the Union address.

Underresourcing other elements of power is most damaging to soldiers, sailors, airmen, and Marines. Soldiers should not be sewage experts in Iraq or build the justice system, but they must because no other department produces the expertise and the people in enough quantity to do the job. We are not a country at war, or even a government at war, we are just a military at war. Strengthening the ability of other agencies to contribute would reduce the demands on our military. If winning the war on terror depends finally on coordinated civilian-military activity, as it surely does, we should not ask our military to continue sacrificing if we are not willing to shoulder the civilian burden of completing the mission.

The final reason to look with a jaundiced eye on the size of U.S. defense spending is that its politics are unsustainable. The decades-long timelines for recruiting and training talented service men and women, developing technologies, and procuring weapons require stability in budgeting. Spikes in defense spending initiate programs that must later be cancelled at great cost to the taxpayer.

Conclusion

Military power remains an important currency in the international order, certainly with our adversaries. Our dominance of conventional warfare has ensured that no state or organization could fight us conventionally and have any reasonable prospect of success. Our weakness in orchestrating the different means of power in Iraq has demonstrated an enormous vulnerability for enemies to exploit. Using force badly not only dishonors the sacrifices our military makes, it also devalues the currency of military force. For if countries and organizations believe we cannot apply our military power effectively to protect and advance our interests, confidence in us as a guarantor will decline and challenges to our interests will rise—the cost of maintaining the international order will rise substantially for us. America has work to do in rebuilding confidence in our ability to use force effectively.

If we are going to use military force to achieve difficult and complex political effects, we must have the ability as a government to carry out comprehensive, integrated strategies with political, economic, social, and military elements sequenced in time and intensity of application, with constant reevaluation and recalibration of effect. The American government does not currently have that ability. Not even close. We are overinvested in defense spending and underinvested in the other essential elements of government activity. As a political community, then, we have two choices if we want to use military force effectively: we can either realign the resourcing and conduct of national security policy to give us greater capability, or we can limit our uses of force to direct, first-order effects of breaking things and killing people. The range of choice is binary; all other alternatives lead to the kind of failures we have seen in Iraq.

CHAPTER 5

Alliances and Institutions

★ ★ ★

To the extent that there has been a relaxation in concern about American power recently, it results from states believing that American power has crested and we have begun an inevitable decline. Our failure to deliver a stable and democratic Iraq, the incredible productivity of China and India's economies, the president's abysmal approval ratings, the continued worrying growth of our fiscal and trade deficits, the horror at the deprivation and suffering on display in the aftermath of Hurricane Katrina all combine to give others the impression of a stumbling colossus, squandering its power and forced to the humbling conclusion that we must move back into the patterns of multilateral behavior most other states are comfortable with. Those expectations are probably misplaced, both as an assessment of American power and as a prediction of our engagement with other countries and international institutions.

If American advantages remain durable as globalization advances, we and the rest of the world will be stuck with America as hegemon for another forty or fifty years. It may not be what many states and societies want, but absent a catastrophic discontinuity, the vectors of power will continue to deliver it. In fact, rather than becoming more like other states as we struggle to overcome our internal problems and other challengers rise, it may well be that America becomes more successful than, and more different from, other states. The slope of the lines representing our power and that of other states may diverge further than at present, increasing our power relative to others'.

Moreover, pessimistic analyses place too much weight on the present setbacks in Iraq and difficulties of the current administration. The fundamental strengths of American political culture and the American economy give us much greater resiliency than they credit. Other states and societies would have to be more resilient, faster adapting, more magnetic, more capable along a wide range of political, cultural, economic, and social factors than we are for the United States to decline. It merits repeating that the United States came to dominate the international order as globalization advanced because the very things that make one successful domestically in America are the things that make one successful in the political, economic, and cultural milieu of a globalizing economy. Our power is so enormous because we dominate through attraction and innovation, and the elements of our power reinforce each other. The time and transition costs are substantial for other states and societies to catch up, and their succeeding would require America's failing to adapt during prolonged competition, which is unlikely.

There are drawbacks to hegemony, some being that others impute that our actions cause many problems, expect that we will solve every problem, and blame us for problems that remain unsolved. This dynamic is already apparent in the way Europeans talk about our failing to put enough pressure on Israel to force its acquiescence to a peace deal or behave as though U.S. choices rather than Iranian choices were advancing the Iranian nuclear program. Not only do others not adequately share the burden of producing the common good of security in the international order, they often consider a critique of our work as a sufficient contribution. It is Mancur Olsen's "free rider" problem, only worse, because our efforts are often actually hindered by those whose interest is in achieving what we are engaged in.[1]

If one were to design a set of international institutions and alliances for another half century of American dominance in the international order, the current relations are certainly not what would be envisioned. The United Nations is too powerful as a legitimating body and too irresponsible as an acting body. NATO requires enormous American effort to produce the modest political and military activity it undertakes. We are overinvested in some relationships that were created for earlier threats and have allowed the constraints of those relations to be extrapolated into new circumstances in ways that impede our management of cur-

---

1. Mancur Olsen, *The Logic of Collective Action: Public Goods and the Theory of Groups* (Cambridge, MA: Harvard University Press, 1965).

rent threats. We are underinvested in relationships that have potential to pull rising powers into positive-sum activity and encourage friendly middle-range powers to take leadership roles. We are too much concerned about activity by institutions we are not members of, and too little concerned about the danger of capable contributors to international peace and security remaining passive.

How, then, might we engage the countries and institutions to better align our relationships with the demands of the current international order? Our ability to foster reform in existing institutions will remain limited as long as there exists no competition for our participation: we should work to create a market in which states and institutions compete for opportunities to have our involvement and support. We need to develop a strategy that invests others more in solving problems and creates new multilateral opportunities—and we need to manage the migration to those new relations with the lowest possible transition costs. American power may have broad enough shoulders to carry the rest of the international order, but even if this were possible, it is unclear why it would be preferable. Unless others are encouraged and empowered and rewarded for taking responsibility to solve problems where they can contribute, we will be expected to solve every problem, and that is a recipe for exhaustion and resentment, both domestically and internationally.

Current Institutions and Allies

Why should we not want an international order in which other states and multilateral institutions carry more of the burden of solving problems, when there are clearly more problems than the United States has an interest in solving? Three arguments are advanced: first, that problems will not get solved anyway, because none except us has the ability to solve them; second, that others will not solve the problems as we would; and third, that we will diminish our power if we allow others to grow in capability. All are inaccurate.

The first argument posits that international institutions are irredeemably impotent, collections of allies either feckless or well intentioned but underresourced, and therefore only the United States has the ability to affect problems. This assertion is patently false. The European Union has proven itself expert at providing membership and trade incentives to positively shape the behavior of countries once considered Europe's periphery. The Organization of American States has become a bulwark of support for democracy in Latin America. The Organization for African Unity has deployed peacekeeping troops to many of the continent's troubled areas and performed creditably. The International Monetary Fund has championed sound economic policies (and some bad ones) and worked with faltering economies to straighten out fundamentals. The United Nations, the institution most derided for incapacity, is actually very good at quite a number of things:

- Identifying health risks and providing through the World Health Organization the vaccines and other medications that, in this age of easy travel, reduce our own vulnerability to pandemic disease.
- Improved understanding of the nuclear safety and weapons capability of nations through its subordinate International Atomic Energy Agency, which has conducted inspections that not only provide us with essential information for our own intelligence assessments but save us the effort of conducting all those inspections of states whose programs we are not concerned about.
- Encouraging and funding the national contributions of military forces and the conduct of Chapter 6 (neutral interposition) missions between formerly warring parties.
- Imposing, and then embarrassing nations into honoring, sanctions.
- Drawing attention to shameful abuses of human rights.

That the UN is also unquestionably bad at some things—preventing aggression, conduct of Chapter 7 (enforcement) missions, acting when there is no Security Council consensus, taking unpopular positions when they would advance peace and security, quickly pulling together capable multinational military forces—should not diminish our appreciation for what it does well. This simply means we should either adapt the institution so that it can do better, or use it only for what it can do well. The UN is a large, sloppy, inefficient, sometimes even corrupt collection of self-interested states using their diplomatic offices to shift blame from their own actions or inaction. Fair enough. But it is also a useful tool, if we wield it with lots of attention and some skill (as, for example, the British commit enormous effort to great effect in doing).

Much of the criticism of the UN is more deservedly leveled at member nations rather than at the institution. We often push problems into the UN framework when we care too little to solve them nationally (genocide in Rwanda and Darfur come to mind) and then strike admirable poses about our own high-mindedness or commitment while bemoaning the UN's incapacity. We often allow the process to churn on unproductively rather than use our national leverage to produce solutions through sequential bilateral deals. We often blame the UN for mistakes we make nationally (military operations in Somalia in 1992) rather than take responsibility where we have done poorly. We often ascribe our diplomatic failure to persuade others to support us to an implacable institutional hostility to American power. We publicize the UN's worst excesses without trumpeting its successes. Such politicization erodes support for the institution in ways that cannot be easily reconstituted when we need it to validate our approach or take a share in solving problems.

We seem to labor under the mistaken assumption these days that countries must come to the UN's New York headquarters with open minds and pure hearts for achieving the common good (by which we mean advancement of our own interests). Not only do we not have that United Nations, we never have had that United Nations. It is a malarial swamp of narrow national interest advanced by buying the acquiescence of other states and enrobing the outcome in the ermine mantle of the International Community—but no nation benefits as much from that process as does the United States of America. As the guarantor of the international order, it is manifestly in our interest to have the UN engaged in building awareness and extracting effort from others. We fund peacekeeping operations to stabilize a fragile peace because we otherwise would be expected to do so with our own forces, we establish rules that attempt to proscribe behavior because we will be expected to prevent or punish such behavior, we support appointments for countries whose help we have received or are in need of because we are investing in future influence, we acquiesce in activity that is meaningless to us because it provides important validation for countries that have less freedom of action than we do.

Another dirty little secret about international institutions is the extent to which Americans staff and control them. We may not be the face of the World Health Organization, but most doctors constituting the

WHO's research and response teams are Americans. No one doubts that the International Monetary Fund and World Bank are extensions of the American Treasury Department. Publicity surrounding the International Atomic Energy Agency (IAEA) inspection teams in Iraq revealed the extent to which we often provide the IAEA with well-trained staff who are also contributing intelligence officers. We exact substantial activity from international institutions through the capable people we provide as what the military terms "force multipliers"—small contributions that make the larger effort more easily attained.

NATO provides perhaps the best example of, quite literally, force multipliers: we pay 25 percent of the common costs of NATO operations, with nations paying the costs of their contributions. The trajectory of our force contribution to NATO operations in the Balkans began at around 25 percent, dropped to 15 percent after a couple of years, spiked during the Kosovo air campaign, then dropped to about 5 percent of the total force today. NATO even handed the mission off to the European Union, ending our common funding contribution. For about 15 percent of the total effort across a decade, we gained stability in the Balkans, time for political changes to take hold (led by the United Nations), and responsibility for solving the problem, a responsibility now taken by others who are exercising it well. The process has not been without its difficulties, especially as it was the first out-of-area deployment for the alliance and the first attempt to lash together NATO, the EU, and the UN: the dual-key approval system between NATO and the UN was both aggravating and ineffectual; military forces were used in untenable circumstances (political leaders believing their actions neutral because humanitarian, not acknowledging that preventing the Serbs from starving Croats out of villages affected the outcome of the war); NATO and the EU still prize institutional competition above practical linkages. But given that the Balkan wars are problems at the margin of American interests, it is good stewardship to have others take responsibility for their resolution rather than commit the predominance of effort and resources ourselves. This has set a precedent that may be extended to Afghanistan in time.

Despite our considerable ability to shape institutions and make them more effective, we Americans often act as though institutions are the problem rather than the means we could use to affect problems. The

Bush administration's attitude toward international treaties mirrors the difficulty: the administration was concerned that the treaties created a false sense of security by allowing participating countries to congratulate themselves on their virtue, without capturing the nonparticipating countries whose behavior was dangerous. So it doesn't matter if fifty-six countries sign the Comprehensive Test Ban Treaty—they aren't the countries we'd be worried about conducting nuclear tests—but having the treaty in force lulls governments into complacency. The logic has merit, but only in that the treaty is insufficient in itself. That is, the concern shouldn't be an argument against the treaty, just against considering the treaty the entirety of the solution. To reject the treaty implies that corralling those fifty-six well-behaved countries has no value, when in fact it establishes a norm and gives standing for the initial participants to sanction the cheaters and ones who opt out. Rather than refusing the Comprehensive Test Ban Treaty as inadequate for preventing clandestine nuclear programs, we should have used it as the foundation for the next stage of activity.

We have lost confidence in our ability to make a winning case for our interests, in our ability to craft deals that give both sides gains. Can a nation that thrives in a constant election cycle really be disadvantaged in making its case in a large public forum? The self-interested behavior of states in international organizations has not changed. What has changed is American willingness to trudge through the hard work of building consensus one nation at a time, one deal at a time, giving all the credit to the countries whose votes delivered the outcome. Our hegemony has seduced us into believing we no longer need to work the corridors and orchestrate that headquarters work with efforts in national capitals and domestic media markets to charm and pressure governments into agreeing to deals that protect and advance our interests because we are willing to help them protect and advance theirs. If we are to be effective at the United Nations, we must return to the small-ball approach of solving others' problems in order to gain incremental improvements in support for ours.

The first step in revising our alliances is to accept institutions as the marketplace for buying and selling influence. It is an uncomfortable description, but we are affecting little change by asserting our preferences as uniquely virtuous. If we walked into headquarters buildings with the

mindset of estimating what it will cost to achieve our objectives, and
having made the calculation of what we are willing to offer states for
their support, we would be in better trade space.

Multilateralism without institutions. The first argument against international institutions is right in its narrowest sense: the UN cannot preserve international peace and stability. Only power credibly threatened
and used can do that. But the UN can make it less costly for America to
preserve international peace and stability, and that is an important contribution we are undervaluing. Even if we are the force solving the problems, it is in our interests to have an international institution appearing
to lead. In many instances it would be too discrediting for a government
to permit national intrusion in its difficulties, but that government may
allow an international institution to intervene. In many instances we
don't want to own a problem by solving it nationally, and an international institution spreads the burden. Instead of vilifying international
institutions, we should match their functions to their abilities, as any
manager would in staffing a team, and look for opportunities to use the
institutions in ways that develop their competence to perform the functions we want them to undertake.

Given that we alone are powerful enough to act without international support and in contravention of international norms, we will get
extra credit for being institution builders and exemplars. One of the reasons the UN was considered favorable ground for the United States in the
1950s and 1960s was that we benefited from our support for decolonization. As more countries came into the UN, they were reflexively sympa-
thetic to our concerns; this was also true for new NATO members. Since
we are not a status quo power, we have an affinity for the upstart, which
we could capitalize on to give those whose rising power is marginalized
in current institutions other chances. Recent U.S.–China bilateral economic summits are a good start in this direction; supporting revision of
the Group of 8 (G-8) to reflect current economic heavyweights would be
even more valued by the Chinese. The challenge, of course, is finding
institutional reforms that do not alienate those from whom something
will be taken. We have had reasonable success in NATO by figuring out
which countries we wanted admitted, and then ensuring criteria were
devised that included them.

A major United Nations reform effort failed in 2006. The United States had ambitions for the UN to denounce terrorism, reform membership of the Human Rights Commission, and adopt reforms advocated by the High-Level Panel on Threats, Challenges, and Change.[2] We failed on all counts, and the UN is a poorer place for it. The 2006 reform effort is a case study in how not to engage international institutions. Our overbearing approach reinforced all the negative stereotypes: Ambassador Bolton symbolized the unyielding face of American dominance; threats to bring the house down if reform wasn't adopted reinforced the inaccurate assumption in the United States that we don't gain from the institution as it is; our metric for reform was efficiency, an objective much less important to others than to us. Our insistence on reform on our terms cost us the adoption of terror language manifestly in our interests. Buy-in by other countries should be our goal for activity at the United Nations. However, coming so soon after Iraq, with an ambassador more comfortable in the role of thundering Old Testament prophet than emollient facilitator, circumstances were hardly ideal. And our failings do not erase the fact that the institution is not contributing nearly so well as it should to peace and security.

Former Secretary General Kofi Annan admitted that the UN needs to make itself more useful or become irrelevant to the security equation. Relevance is exactly the hook on which to hang reform, because it gives the institution and its most committed members an incentive to act. If we have alternatives to UN action, we create a market for institutional supervision that would give the UN incentives to become more useful, if only to protect its market share, so to speak. The NATO alliance created one alternative by using force in Kosovo; the Proliferation Security Initiative and other collectives organized by the Bush administration are amassing precedents that will marginalize the UN unless it takes a more active and creative approach to confronting the problems of international peace and security. Our goal should be to develop myriad focused collectives that solve countries' problems, can expand membership to become broadly international, and give countries willing to take initiative rewards for sharing the burden of guaranteeing the international order with us.

2. UN High-Level Panel on Threats, Challenges and Change, "A More Secure World: Our Shared Responsibility," United Nations, 2005.

Given that America has generally good relations with rising powers, we should invest more in cooperatively solving their problems to show we aren't hostile to their rise, and since in most instances their problems are our problems. For example, we and the Chinese are concerned about freedom of navigation in the Straits of Malacca, which should offer an opportunity for collaborative patrolling. It needn't be solely with China; we have established security relationships with many of the surrounding countries, and those countries are anxious about China's military spending and activism. It behooves us to be the fulcrum on which cooperation rests; we have a common problem, and our established allies would be relieved to have the prospect of positive engagement.

An activist agenda with more partners would somewhat take the sting out of a realignment of U.S. alliances to invest less in Europe as a whole. There are European countries that are critically important as allies. However, there is a repositioning occurring in the international order wherein some states that have been traditional U.S. allies are less willing to shoulder the burden of the new security problems that we are most alarmed by. The Clinton administration acknowledged this in 1994 with the creation of a Quad composed of the UK, France, Germany, and the United States to build a core of NATO agreement. We need to make these changes gracefully, honoring the existing rituals for extended periods while countries adapt to the changes. It may increase our patience to recall that our country, too, may one day be on the receiving end of diminished effort by a hegemon.

The proclivities of some countries align more closely with ours, and these countries are already forming an inner circle of *primus inter pares:* Britain, Australia, the Netherlands, Denmark, Poland, China, possibly Sweden. Canada has traditionally been among those closest to us, and its brave work in Afghanistan may well return it to that position as the searing experience of fighting there brings our perspectives on the world back into closer alignment. These countries are "comprised in the fore-rank of our articles," as Shakespeare's Henry V said of his Catherine. They are the countries we will turn to first, that we will invest in most heavily in preserving integral intelligence and military cooperation, that we should view as trusted agents to lead the regional and international efforts that we would assist to ensure their success.

Emboldening and ensuring the success of these countries would increase their stature, and therefore their potential to lead and contribute. It would also take the focus off American hegemony to have them, rather than us, in the lead. It is critically important that the United States privilege and reward these countries to keep the support for their governments domestically viable. Prime Minister Tony Blair suffered irrecoverably from the British public's believing he had gained too little influence over President Bush despite Britain's participation and support in the Iraq War.

Canada may remain somewhat outside the inner circle, instead being among those countries with an understandable domestic focus but nonetheless having special claims on us because their domestic problems are our problems. Mexico is in this category, and also Colombia. In each case, governments are struggling against long odds to change their societies in positive ways, and their domestic success is the key to managing issues we are concerned about: immigration, drug trafficking, border control. Mexico probably paid the biggest price of any country for the diversion of effort in the U.S. government after September 11. Problems the Bush administration had a natural affinity for solving were washed away by the more immediate pressures of confronting terrorism.

One unhelpful idea for advancing international cooperation is a concert of democracies. Modeled on the Concert of Europe that balanced power among Germany, Austria, Britain, France, and Russia for a century, this approach would circle the wagons of the world's eighty-some democracies to mandate actions that advance our common interests. It is a popular idea, curiously so, given its obvious deficiencies: first, that it excludes countries we are working very hard to make into responsible international stakeholders, such as China; second, that we already have regional institutions incorporating most of these countries that could mandate action; third, that the countries most opposed to U.S. actions to advance democracy are often the established Western democracies; and fourth, its faulty premise that countries with common values are willing to acknowledge common interests and act on them. We would be providing one more grandstand from which the French and Germans could give pious speeches against our policies, while discouraging countries like China that are thirsting for the status of inclusion in negotiations and opportunities to show their constructive contributions.

Why NATO Is Better

The NATO alliance is the only international institution that generates any warmth of affection from Americans. It began as the cold war bulwark against Soviet expansion, the collection of our closest friends; turned with surprising grace to enfold a unified Germany and to reassure newly democratic (and strongly pro-American) states in Europe; went first to the Balkans and now to Afghanistan to fight on behalf of our common interests. The alliance imaginatively created new mechanisms, such as the Partnership for Peace, that delayed decision on new members while setting standards for admission that gave incentives for positive domestic change, and the NATO-Russia Council, that gave Russia special status to compensate somewhat for its formerly subjugated partners becoming NATO allies. The promise in the North Atlantic Treaty's Article V that "an attack on one will be considered an attack on all" was invoked for the first time after September 11, and allied aircraft patrolled American airspace. There is even affection at the base of allied disgruntlement that NATO did not play a larger role in retaliation against the Taliban: our friends wanted to be of assistance. Most forces in the Iraq coalition come from NATO countries. NATO is, as former Secretary General George Robertson likes to say, "the only standing coalition in the world," an organization in which members are predisposed to assist the United States in ways they often would not be bilaterally (Greece's support for the war in Kosovo, for example, is difficult to imagine outside a NATO framework).

What makes NATO successful where other institutions are not? It has a narrow focus on security, with elaborate organizational practices that reinforce the focus and build common understanding. Its Article V guarantees American military forces for the defense of all members' territories and the bonus of American attention at the highest levels of government several times a year. The cost, to Europeans, is our constant harangue to spend more on defense and not lose the ability to fight alongside American forces.

For America, NATO is our best bet for sustaining capable military forces in the countries most able to help us. NATO allies have the most proficient military forces in the world, buy sophisticated equipment, and train to common standards. The constant practice of interoperability in NATO's Integrated Military Command ensures NATO standards can be adopted for coalition wars, reducing the difficulties experienced in most military coalitions. The alliance has a history of—in fact, a genius for—compromise solutions that bind the members together by simultaneously assenting to contradictory positions (for example, the 1979 Dual-Track decision that deployed intermediate-range nuclear weapons while advocating negotiations on their elimination).

NATO's success contrasts with the UN's failure in several important ways: we control its membership, excluding querulous or anti-American states (unless they were founding members, like France); it makes decisions only by unanimity, and thus there is no question of outcomes invidious to our interests; there is a strong sense of shared values, beyond the immediate defense obligations, that prejudice outcomes positively; and arguments about respective contributions have agreed metrics (percentage of gross domestic product spent on defense, deployable military forces).

It is also true, however, that all of NATO's affectionate entanglements have been insufficient to produce a common approach to terrorism, proliferation, how to deal with a thuggish Russia, or what to do about crises in Iraq, Lebanon, and Iran. Besides our strongest supporters, it often contains our most vehement detractors. It has done nothing useful to help in Iraq except agree to train Iraqi troops, but only in very small numbers and only outside Iraq. It bravely stepped up to the mission in Afghanistan but is badly underresourcing the security needs of achieving our objectives. NATO is the most overtly pro-American institution, the one most adapted to the new threats, the one we invest the greatest amount of time and effort to shape to our needs, and it still falls well short of being a true partner for the United States.

If even NATO cannot be relied on to contribute significantly, perhaps the opponents of working through multinational institutions should carry the argument. Perhaps our interests would be advanced further by pulling together coalitions of the willing, as Secretary Rumsfeld advocated. For the United States, the advantages of working without an institutional safety net would be substantial. Europeans often have a

Eurocentric view of the world inadequately sensitive to the concerns of countries most affected by crises in Asia or the Middle East. Our opponents could not block bilateral deals they were not a party to. We would spend much less time on losing propositions, allowing redirection of our diplomatic efforts to more likely contributors. We would have more leverage with individual allies that are contributors, as they would not have strength in numbers or the chance to avoid detection behind others' concerns. The terms on which they participated in operations would likely revert to the superior U.S. standard, with fewer compromises to allied equipment or doctrine. We could choose only allies willing to make operationally significant military contributions, without being imposed on by "contributions" that take more effort than doing the work ourselves.

NATO advocates often suggest that there is a cost-effectiveness in diplomacy conducted through the alliance, one-stop shopping for delivering a passel of contributors. In practice, agreement at NATO is generally a product of extensive negotiations in national capitals as well as Brussels, so it is unclear whether ending the Brussels negotiations would be a net gain or loss. What is clear is that the routine interaction in NATO military staffs and headquarters helps substantially in building effective military coalitions. The strengths and weaknesses of national militaries are well known through the review of defense plans and observation of unit performance. NATO's top military commanders, one European (chairman of the NATO Military Committee) and two Americans (supreme allied commanders for operations and for transformation), have the knowledge to build force packages making the best use of available national forces in ways and with an alacrity no other American combatant commanders would be able to match.

There would also be costs in allowing NATO to atrophy into the organization it was originally designed in 1949 to be—one that promised political solidarity, with no supporting military infrastructure to undergird the deal. Social welfare spending, threat perceptions, and a receding appreciation for military force as an element of statecraft would quite likely combine to reduce defense spending in most European countries. EU advocates claim publics will be willing to support higher spending for European operations, but this claim remains unsubstantiated these sixteen years after the great leap forward in the European Security and

Defense Policy. Without a prospect of collective military action, both the willingness of countries to contribute capabilities and the ability of the institution to piece them into a militarily effective force would decline, aggravating the "free rider" problem (both for NATO and the EU) and increasing the burden for large military contributors. The United States would lose interest in the institution, since it would be solving so few of the problems with which we are engaged, reducing the political value of it to Europeans and Americans alike. Goodwill, difficult to quantify but apparent in individual states' squeamishness about being the spoiler of the unanimity and collective will of so many others, would diminish as a force pushing states to agreement. American supporters would probably have less leverage in influencing other allies, since there would be no "ruining NATO" wolf cry to spur European contributions. Supporting U.S. policies without NATO would also, as the Iraq War demonstrated for Britain, complicate the ambitions of the allies that support us. The United States could seem to allied publics more like a dominating power imposing on its vassal states without the edge-softening tedium of constant compromise in NATO. If Europeans are not engaged in solving problems, it will aggravate their tendency to offer criticism of American efforts rather than substantive contributions of their own.

A pure coalitions-of-the-willing strategy, then, frees America from the burden of alliance compromise where allies are contributing little, but sacrifices important political and military capital in the medium to long term; this argues for sustaining pressure for NATO to be more active but also for changing the terms of that activity. We should work hard to retain an esprit de corps for collective action in NATO, pushing the horizon of that action outward to more closely align with the problems America is worried about. We should not, however, simply extend the NATO practices we agreed to for the defense of European territories to circumstances in which Europeans are contributors but not principal stakeholders: it actually matters more what Pakistan thinks about closing the Afghan border than it matters what Europeans think; it actually matters more what Israelis think about the Shebaa farms than what Europeans think. But we still conduct consultations as though Europeans deserve the bulk of effort and weight in our choices. They have a right to a preponderance of influence when it is their own defense we are mutually conducting; they do not necessarily deserve that influence when they are not principal stakeholders, but we are. Therefore, as the United States continues to adapt NATO, we should make two important changes to our transatlantic policy: consultations with non-European participation, and creating the means to plug a NATO module into broader coalition operations.

We are in a near-constant state of consultations with Europeans. What we seldom do is consult with Europeans where talks include non-Europeans. There is the Middle East Quartet of the United States, the EU, Russia, and the UN, and regular U.S. talks with force contributors in Afghanistan and Iraq, but for the most part, when we consult with Europeans, other stakeholders in security are not present. Even on Iran, where Europeans have admirably taken a leading role, we talk among ourselves, and Europe with the Iranians, but too little with the governments of Saudi Arabia, Turkey, Iraq, and other friendly countries that are affected by Iran's nuclear ambitions. This is a mistake, for it encourages Europeans to believe their views are paramount in shaping our actions. By holding consultations with small groups of regional stakeholders and Europeans, we give our European allies a better sense of the other forces shaping U.S. views and actions and expose our European allies to expectations that they will contribute to solving problems.

As one example, transatlantic policy-planning discussions would be greatly enriched by the routine participation of Chinese or Indian counterparts. One recent experience of including the Indian and Chinese governments left Europeans wondering whether their support for "effective multilateralism" might not be misplaced if rising powers aligned with American views—they had assumed European attitudes would be the center of gravity. On many critical issues, the United States is closer in its views to the directly affected countries than to European views, because we often have defense commitments that involve us more in the problem. While Europeans certainly don't lack in sophisticated understanding of the world, they do often underestimate how constrained U.S. choices are by our obligations to others, or how intractable countries can be when their own security is at stake. Europeans tend to believe that if only the United States would pay attention to a problem, we could solve it.

Expanding the circle of participation in this way runs the risk of tilting other allies' views more toward that of Europeans, but it gives too little credit to the self-interest of the Japanese, Jordanians, Australians, and Argentinians and other American partners to believe exposure to European arguments will bend their policies beyond our influence. Besides, we should not imagine them innocent of such exposure whether or not we are participating in the discussion.

Consulting on a "Europeans plus" format would also give countries whose influence is increasing structured opportunities to be in the elite rank of our closest partners. It might seem torturous for countries to endure the nonstop transatlantic negotiation, but all would view it as conveying status to them. It would accustom them to the exchange of ideas, tough bargaining, and positive-sum outcomes that characterize the transatlantic relationship. It might even encourage their participation in negotiating teams or military coalitions. We could do much worse than having rising powers aspire to relations with the United States comparable to those of our European allies.

The second shift in our transatlantic approach is directed at the nuts and bolts of military cooperation. It would be to create a process for bundling NATO forces into a single unit and having the supreme allied commander Europe (SACEUR) negotiate the terms of use for the force with his American counterpart responsible for the operation. This would solve several problems. Europeans complained during the Afghanistan and Iraq operations that U.S. commanders knew too little of their capabilities to make good use of their forces. They were excluded from operations they might have contributed to, and from the planning for them—"treated like just any other country," in the refrain of many sitting unproductively in the coalition trailer park in Tampa.[3] The complaint is partly about status, and partly about substance. American commanders not accustomed to working with NATO allies understandably don't have time to become experts on the Danish Air Force or German communications systems, and so won't build a plan to which they are integral.

But we do have an American commander expert on the European mil-

3. Restrictions on intelligence sharing do not permit allies except the British and Australians (who are considered American in the application of the intelligence category U.S. Eyes Only during operations) access to classified U.S. areas. Countries contributing forces to Operations Enduring Freedom and Iraqi Freedom were thus housed in portable trailers at the U.S. Central Command, an indignity resented by many NATO allies.

itaries: the SACEUR. Moreover, as a senior American four-star general, he also has influence in the policy development and military planning that no European commander could. The SACEUR would be the most effective advocate of European concerns and contributions, and if he were deputized to recruit participation and package forces, it would dramatically reduce the workload on the combatant commander in charge of the war and produce a better military contribution. The SACEUR could negotiate with the combatant commander on specific missions that NATO forces could then take responsibility for carrying out, negotiate with nations for force contributions, have his planning staff match national strengths with elements of the mission requirements, and bring the force package back to NATO and the combatant command for approval. In military terms, the SACEUR would become a subordinate commander with the operational control of national forces conducting agreed missions.

The practice builds on NATO post–cold war adaptations, such as the combined joint task force concept (which aimed to provide deployable cells of staffers to out-of-area operations), the NATO Reaction Force (which keeps a small force in high operational readiness, identifying necessary enablers for European forces not accustomed to deployment and conveying the alliance's best practices into national militaries), and Allied Command Transformation (charged with fostering innovation and keeping interoperability among NATO forces as transformation advances at different speeds in allied militaries). NATO could even set up standing staff elements in U.S. military commands, such as the U.S. Pacific Command, for allied familiarity with planning and exercises on a regular basis. It would not obligate nations to participate in specific operations but would provide a way of rapidly pulling together building blocks of national forces into a self-sustaining force that could be plugged into broader coalitions.

This approach would be likely to encounter two obstacles: opposition to a "tool box" NATO, and the preference of nations for bilateral over multilateral relations with the United States. The first is easy to dismiss but hard to overcome, as it concerns NATO theology. Medieval Christian prelates had nothing on contemporary NATO experts in the obsession with obscure points of doctrine. The French and Belgian governments oppose NATO being considered a functional means of achieving military cooperation—which they believe runs against the alliance being a "political NATO"—and therefore drag their feet on building practical ways to organize and deliver military forces. The alliance spent six months of negotiations in 1991 over whether NATO was "an" essential foundation of European security or "the" essential foundation of European security. There is no reasonable argument that can overcome the objection made by the French and Belgian governments; every conceivable formula has been tried and rejected. The objection can only be placated, and only by the application of large doses of presidential attention bilaterally administered to the French. It is the only formula that has proven successful, but it has delivered results: the French have opposed nearly every practical adaptation of NATO's military structures but have acceded once much bilateral effort was expended at the highest political levels.[4] Seeing that our effort builds goodwill with other allies, and with French acceptance, the Belgian objection will usually be withdrawn.

The second concern splits Europe in a different way, isolating those allies with the closest relationship to the United States. Establishing a NATO module diminishes the influence of individual allies who would have been included anyway based on their national contribution, especially Britain, but also the Netherlands, Denmark, Poland, and Romania. In other words, it penalizes the best-contributing allies. It does not necessarily follow that those countries would prefer not to have an identifiable NATO contribution—for some it would ease their inner-European difficulties to be less visible in bilateral relations with the United States or to embed their forces in a larger NATO operation. But others certainly would have such a contribution: France participates in many activities of the U.S. Pacific Command but may well oppose extending NATO's reach that far. NATO has long experience with this kind of problem, however, and can usually circumvent objections by having both NATO and national contributions (for example, the United States has always maintained a separate chain of command through the U.S. European

4. The two adaptations they did not attempt to restrain were the NATO Reaction Force and the establishment of Allied Command Transformation. The French government probably judged they would benefit from a close understanding of transformation as it is occurring in U.S. forces, and that other allies (especially the UK) would have bilateral opportunities that would endanger French influence over the development of standards in EU defense cooperation if they did not allow a NATO role.

Command so that NATO objections could not forestall operations). Allies can then choose which venue best suits their tactical objectives in a particular operation without preventing collective work.

Gaining agreement will, as usual in NATO, take considerable patience and effort. But it poses the prospect of greater contributions from the countries most able and often most willing to help in U.S. operations and of organizing those contributions to better effect while reducing the burden on the combatant commander planning for and executing the war. It sustains a common NATO force within a broader coalition, both using and adapting the institution in ways that give allies incentives to cooperate and to contribute.

A Sustainable Strategy

The discussion of changes to our transatlantic relations leads toward a more general approach to conducting alliance relations in our time of hegemony: emboldening others to act by underwriting their success. The magnitude of our power inclines other states to expect us to manage problems, when it is in our interests to spread the responsibility among states and encourage them to become willing and able to help.

We are now too preoccupied with the notion of strong states challenging our influence. We worry that China contributing troops to UN missions in Lebanon and Haiti presages a China that will supplant us, or that an EU agitating to take over NATO missions in the Balkans is an ungrateful slap in the face after sixty years of American protection. We ought to be much more worried about the opposite problem: an international order in which states are unwilling to step forward and contribute to solutions. That is the more likely outcome and the international order most invidious to American interests, for we will be expected to solve every problem; states that could contribute will not, and we will be confronted with criticism from states that run no risks and therefore underestimate the difficulty of solving international problems.

The Bush administration began in 2001 focused on four elements in international relations: (1) cementing positive relations between ourselves and other great powers (Russia and Europe); (2) preparing for rising powers, whether hostile or friendly (China, India); (3) turning back the tide of international agreements unduly constraining to American interests (Kyoto, the International Criminal Court); (4) building partnerships of common interests with overlooked countries (Mexico, Australia, Poland). The administration considered American policies overinvested in relations with established European powers, entangled in problems not meriting our involvement (the Balkans, Middle East peace), indulgent to the point of irresponsibility with status quo international institutions and agreements (the UN, the Anti-Ballistic Missile Treaty, basing of U.S. forces in Europe and Korea and Japan), and failing to take opportunities for dramatic change (Russia, Mexico). It was a bold change in direction, a pistol shot in the middle of a concert, as Stendhal would say, announcing our comfort with hegemony and taking a harder edge to making others acknowledge and adapt to it, as well.[5] It was also an important effort to realign our international relations with our international interests. That it was carried out in ways that skyrocketed the cost of achieving those objectives does not invalidate the objectives.

The problem with brazen declarations, of course, is that while they play well domestically, especially with Americans in the Jacksonian tradition, they cause alarm internationally. As the hegemon, the United States no longer has the luxury of a domestic media market that is not also carefully watched internationally, so there are costs for an American president not accounting for how key international audiences will react to our domestic politics. The rewards of a clear strategy eruditely argued are that it can be savored by experts, handed down through the government to set priorities, easily understood by a largely inattentive public, and not misinterpreted by enemies. The drawback is that it reduces the likelihood that the states you intend to downgrade or marginalize will consent to changes, and thereby drives up the cost of achieving them.

While being liked is not the point of American foreign policy, being likable reduces the cost of our policies. Moreover, likeable is who we are as a political culture, and a foreign policy not built on our public desire to be seen as a force for good in the world will not long sustain public support. International sympathy in the wake of September 11 gave the United States an opportunity to reassess the high turbulence-to-success ratio of the early Bush administration's approach. Unfortunately, that opportunity came at a time the country was frightened (and therefore

5. Stendahl, *The Charterhouse of Parma,* quoted in Orhan Pamuk, *Snow* (Vintage Books, 2005).

more supportive of executive leadership) and the administration even more convinced of the dangers of continuing the status quo.

Even in these circumstances, the administration might have made very different choices after September 11: pushing the UN forward to lead political engagement with the Taliban, having the UN secretary general and our principal allies always beside the American president as we crafted our response, organizing a UN or NATO military coalition to retaliate, attacking Al Qaeda without overthrowing the Taliban government in Afghanistan, dealing with Al Qaeda as a specific terrorist organization rather than expanding the scope of our activity to a war on terror, focusing effort on improving defensive measures such as point of entry security rather than offensive military action, maintaining a narrow focus on fighting terrorism rather than expanding the political scope of effort to advancing democracy, ensuring that the resourcing of our response didn't give enemies incentives to conduct even more spectacular attacks. These choices would not have had the ringing "challenge of our generation" context the president created, but they provide an alternative vision, a lower-cost and perhaps stronger foundation or strategy for catalyzing change in the international order after September 11.

The second Bush administration has less sharp elbows, partly because of the departure of Secretary of Defense Rumsfeld and UN Ambassador Bolton, and partly because of the recognition that international support is drying up before the grand objectives of President Bush's Wilsonian vision are achieved. We tried and failed to substantially reform the UN. NATO went to Afghanistan but is already questioning the decision and failing to contribute the minimum force levels. Iraq has been predominantly an American operation for some time now. The next round of coalition building will be even more difficult than pulling together support in Iraq, because we have proven ourselves less competent, and the commitment has been of much longer duration and at a higher cost than contributors believed they were signing up for. The tendency of less powerful states to hang back while the hegemon does the hard work will be strongly accentuated by the disappointed expectations of the states assisting in Afghanistan and Iraq.

Accepting variation. If we are to share the burden of maintaining peace and security, we need to develop an approach that encourages other states to take a larger share of responsibility. Fledgling attempts have been made at this in Afghanistan, amid much recrimination, but to largely good effect. NATO states have led provincial reconstruction teams in different areas, with widely different approaches to integrating military force, development assistance, and political engagement. NATO states have also taken responsibility for various sectors of government in Afghanistan, the Italians working with the justice system, the Germans with police training, the United States with development of an Afghan national army. It has worked because Afghanistan's needs are so great that any assistance is an improvement, and states that would not have contributed because they do not support each others' approaches have the latitude to contribute differently. Relaxing the constraints on how states can contribute and giving individual countries leadership roles that make them responsible for achieving results in specific areas encouraged greater contribution.

Innovations in foreign assistance—that is, expecting specific performance results from recipients—have trended this way for several years. Early in the Bush administration, aid was tied to quality of governance through Millennium Challenge Accounts, and most giving from new-generation entrepreneurial charities like the Gates Foundation also requires specific performance standards. What is to some extent new with NATO operations in Afghanistan is holding donors rather than recipients accountable for producing results. This approach measures success by outputs rather than the standard government indicator of inputs but makes it more difficult for donor countries to gain partial credit for having contributed rather than having achieved their objectives. Pressuring contributors is more discreetly done through international institutions, or at least additionally in international institutions, than by the United States directly. That we are the driving force will certainly be known, but the differentials in power make such pressure more likely to be resented when it comes only bilaterally.

Advances in military technology and operational concepts have made it more difficult for countries to contribute significantly to the wars the United States is fighting. This is true whether the war is a high-tech precision engagement across great distances in which mobility, information, and speed of action can substitute for the massing of forces—the war U.S. forces are optimized to fight—or a war requiring force-intensive patrolling. We may not be better in all slices of the military spectrum than other militaries, but we are unquestionably different in how we go about the tasks. We have more sophisticated equipment, have an expeditionary mind-set, and are more conscious of force protection than other militaries.

Our personnel and technological and training edge should not be a good enough reason for America not to find work allied forces can do, and lavish credit on them for doing it. Defense spending has a strong inverse correlation with casualties: countries that spend more money on attracting talented people, training them intensively, and providing them cutting-edge equipment and weapons usually take fewer casualties and inflict fewer unintended friendly force and civilian casualties. This unforgiving arithmetic makes many countries understandably hesitant to share in the fight. It compounds the free rider problem for the United States, since it gives our allies that do not spend as lavishly greater risks in fighting than we will have, while at the same time almost ensuring that our forces will garner more credit. Moreover, it is a problem with long lead-time fixes; it cannot be attended to when a crisis erupts.

Even before our difficulties in Iraq, it was clear America would need allied force contributions if we were required to fight the two nearly simultaneous wars accepted in our defense strategy. In Iraq, it is without question that even if allied governments were concerned about participating in the tasks with greatest risk and requiring greatest sophistication in operations, their forces could have significantly contributed to manpower-intensive tasks, such as monitoring borders, that we have not committed enough forces to undertake.

Our political challenges are persuading allies to sustain spending in peacetime and use their forces aggressively in wartime. One good example is NATO's stress on niche capability programs that will improve national militaries to different bands of high-end capability. Some nations maintain fighter aircraft, others chemical weapons detectors and "consequence management" (cleaning up after their use), others intelligence networks, still others fast patrol boats or mine detectors. As NATO allies can rely on the common defense, they can tailor forces to areas of specialization to create a cumulatively excellent full-spectrum force. By working intensively with allies to shape their forces, as we do in NATO and did somewhat with the coalition in Iraq, we will gain better coalition forces and governments more willing to be contributors.

Besides the high political principles for which governments go to war, other militaries want the opportunity to train with U.S. forces (an opportunity growing scarcer because the operational demands on our forces are so high), the chance to try out our equipment and learn about its technologies, the ability to buy and sell weapons in our market (which is rigidly protectionist for defense articles), the education of sending officers to our war colleges, the status of privileged intelligence and operational relationships with us. The Bush administration garnered lots of angry attention for excluding from these opportunities countries that opposed the war in Iraq or would not sign agreements explicitly refusing to remand Americans to the International Criminal Court. It was unsubtle, often hasty, given the many things on which we want countries' cooperation, but it was not necessarily wrong. We should not buy into a bounding of American power that prohibits us from engaging in punitive actions against countries that choose not to help us advance our interests—there is a perversity in expecting that the country with the greatest power should be the most constrained from using it. We should, however, better calibrate and time-sequence our choices to give incentives to countries to help in the future.

Communications. One place the United States underinvests with respect to shaping other nations' policies is their domestic media markets. Senior American officials will nearly always garner media coverage when traveling; we take those opportunities too infrequently to raise issues for debate on countries' home turf. We are usually good at rewarding friends with visits to the United States or presidential trips, and making high-profile public statements condemning adversaries, but not at using such travel to affect the relations of allied governments with their own publics.[6] Other countries often operate at an asymmetric advantage by sheltering domestic media markets or national policies from having to

6. Secretary Rice's democracy promotion trip to Egypt in 2005 is a laudable exception. By calling on a friendly government to support the American policies directly affecting their domestic political structures and practices, and arguing that these policies served Egyptian as well as American interests, the secretary of state set a standard; it has, however, not been much repeated.

address issues on our terms. Other countries, especially friendly ones, lobby Congress, sponsor think tank events, suggest stories to journalists, and in general work around the American government to shape which issues receive attention and have standing, whereas the United States tends to work with governments, and in capitals or UN and NATO headquarters.

Think of how much more difficult it would have been for Jacques Chirac's government to lead opposition to the war in Iraq if our secretary of state argued in the suburbs of any large French city that we were trying to create a Middle East from which people would not have to emigrate for political freedom and economic opportunity, or for the Schroeder government had the secretary of state gone to Nuremberg to call on Germans to take a special responsibility for helping people suffering under tyrannical governments toward freedom. Instead, the administration focused its efforts on the UN and private bilateral talks and allowed some of its most reckless supporters (Richard Perle comes to mind) to be the voices most allies heard making the case for the Iraq War. Much more could be made of opportunities to engage governments in debate in their own media, but the effort is knowledge, people, and travel intensive—we have to have diplomats and public figures with a sophisticated understanding of the domestic debate in countries, operating in large enough quantity and in enough places to engage debate in terms that will resonate with the local public.

There are two problems with the Bush administration's strategic communications effort: first, it is based on the faulty premise that providing accurate information will diminish opposition to our policies; and second, that as a political culture we are ill-suited to message control. We are playing to our weaknesses rather than our strengths. States and societies are so saturated with information about America that they believe they understand us—what they want is for us to understand them and the effect our policy choices have on their lives.

Hiring Arabists to monitor blogs and correct inaccuracies (as Karen Hughes' office has done) is a good idea, but the small-scale, centralization, and high-level control of such an approach to strategic communications will prevent it from being nearly as successful as it needs to be. We should have hundreds of earnest young diplomats engaged in such activity, giving their own opinions and exchanging ideas, criticizing our government and lauding it as their views accord. This is the Radio Free Europe model of advancing American freedoms by exemplifying them to others rather than explaining them. Instead of attempting to control information, which is antithetical to who we are as a political culture, strategic communications should focus on amplifying the diverse, critically minded, individualistic society we are.

Institutional reform. The discouraging returns on investment for UN reform and need for constant pressure in NATO just to keep allied defense spending at 1.5 percent of national GDP or to get force contributions below but near to the SACEUR's "minimum requirements" can make pessimists out of the most dedicated institutionalists. It is wearying work for which American diplomats do not get nearly enough credit, this continuing to patiently craft consensus and shave margins of disagreement and endure criticism of American policies from countries that are making little contribution to solving the world's problems. The post–World War II institutions were not designed for an international order in which the power of one nation is this predominant, and the special circumstances facing the United States as guarantor of the order often leave us isolated in resisting popular solutions or pressing for unpopular actions that will advance the common good. Other states that cannot deliver institutional outcomes believe that if only we would expend more effort, we could.

All of which makes it tempting to work bilaterally rather than through the UN, NATO, and with other institutions. But while Americans are comfortable with our domestic politics producing the legitimacy for our government actions, most other states are not—they are not comfortable with our politics legitimating our actions, and they are not comfortable with their own politics legitimating their actions. If we are to find ways of encouraging and enabling others to help solve problems to reduce the burden on ourselves, at least in the short term there will need to be a positive institutional component to the undertaking. The relevant question then becomes whether to continue operating with institutions poorly aligned to the new distribution of power in the international order and the threats to peace and security, or to invest in restructuring the institutions.

Three strategies present themselves for restructuring institutions:

the first, to tie our participation to changes; second, to deputize allies to lead the effort with us in support; and third, to create a competitive market for reform by building new institutions. Congress has attempted the first approach during Senator Helms' chairmanship of the Senate Foreign Relations Committee, refusing to pay America's United Nations dues unless reforms were undertaken. The effort served mostly to brand us as obstructing the work of the UN rather than raise awareness of the need for reform in other countries. If this approach were to be attempted again, it should be part of a broader effort to have other countries and their domestic media highlight the need for UN reform. As the burden-shedding beneficiaries of a better-functioning UN, even without the long shadow of our hegemony making us look like bullies, we are ill-positioned to make the case. At a minimum, the United States should corral a few dozen allies to undertake similar rejectionist policies so that our refusal, rather than the need for reform, does not become the story.

The second approach would work bilaterally with allies that have specific expertise, interest, or political market position to affect institutional change. We would privately set up a common bilateral position, have the other country publicly take ownership of the reforms, and support the effort both privately and publicly such that U.S. resources are harnessed to assist in building the success of another state's leadership. For example, the Dutch government, with its exalted history of legal scholarship, could be encouraged to convene a conference to revise the Geneva Conventions for an age of terrorism. Most states acknowledge the problematic nature of applying the Geneva Conventions when terrorists do not distinguish themselves from civilians and expressly target noncombatants. This is a serious shortcoming in the fabric of international law, and the country it most hurts is the United States, as we have the greatest number of military forces engaged. Moreover, it increases the cost to us of guaranteeing international security, where we are not perceived as more virtuously committed to liberal values than the enemies we are fighting.[7]

If we and the Dutch agree on intent, and they know our bottom lines, we should be willing to give them the latitude to navigate while

---

7. Lawrence Freedman makes this case powerfully in *The Revolution in Strategic Affairs* (London: International Institute for Strategic Studies, 2004).

we merely participate. They are a trusted ally and might welcome the opportunity to become synonymous with extending international law to face the frightening new circumstances of wars. It would be a major diplomatic initiative at the forefront of their foreign policy, whereas it would be one of many U.S. undertakings—as witnessed by the fact that the Bush administration has not made the issue a priority despite the damage to American interests that has accrued from other countries' believing we insist on being a law unto ourselves. The Bush administration is not wrong to protest that the Geneva Conventions are inapplicable, but it has imposed an unnecessary cost by not proposing and negotiating a framework that would meet our needs.

An example of how the orchestration has worked was the Australian-led peacekeeping operation in East Timor in 1999. After Somalia, the Clinton administration could not have gained public support for an American-led UN operation, or even American participation. The Australians had interests in stabilizing their neighborhood, supporting the UN, and demonstrating their credentials as an Asian power. With U.S. military support of their operations, and promises we would intervene to assist if Australian efforts began to fail, the Australian government stepped up to a demanding mission and performed it superbly to great credit.

A more tangled but still representative example is European leadership of negotiations over the Iranian nuclear program. In 2003, European governments wanted to prove multilateralism could work in a UN framework and change the confrontational direction of U.S.-Iranian policies. The EU-3 (France, Germany, and the United Kingdom) have committed substantial effort to persuade Iran to accept international engagement, economic opportunity, and energy technology in return for transparency by Iran about its program and an end to fuel reprocessing. They have cajoled Russia some ways out of its complicity (the Russians offered to reprocess the fuel to remove suspicions of Iranian diversion to weapons) and brought both Russia and China to agree to UN sanctions against Iran. That the Iranians have been unwilling to take any number of good deals on offer does not discredit European efforts. It has, in fact, brought Europeans and Americans much closer to a common view on Iran; some European negotiators even complain that the United States has not brandished threats of military attacks on Iran enough, a complaint Americans have not heard from Europe in a very long time. Transatlantic comity may fray over how to proceed beyond tepid sanctions in the face of continued Iranian intransigence, but we are in a better position for having encouraged European leadership on a difficult problem, and they are rightly proud of their achievement.

Starting many bilateral efforts along these lines would give other countries opportunities for leadership and credit, make them more confident of their success, while solving many more problems than we would if America needed to lead every effort. This comes at the cost of others' receiving credit, but surely American power is grounded deeply enough to forgo that benefit, especially since we will be seen as succeeding because of the efforts of our trusted allies.

The third strategy for working through institutions would be simply to construct new ones more aligned to current circumstances and malleable to American interests. The *Onion* parody "U.S. Forms Own UN" makes clear the impossibility of supplanting that institution, but developing other institutions focused on specific issues or deconstructing the global UN approach to regional cooperation have many precedents in trade negotiations as well as foreign policy.[8] The NATO alliance certainly qualifies as such, on both functional and regional grounds, as would the Organization of American States and the bilateral or regional trade treaties that have begun to fill the void as prospects for global trade agreements have receded.

The 2003 Proliferation Security Initiative provides an example of this approach. It builds on appeals by the UN Security Council and G-8 for states to prevent proliferation by gaining agreement from eleven states for exchange of information and the voluntary boarding of their vessels at sea when proliferation is suspected. The UN Law of the Sea Convention prohibits forcible boarding, but the agreement by states to permit it not only allows shipments to be interdicted, it also creates a norm of compromise on sovereignty to control proliferation. The program includes exercises that improve the ability of states to conduct the interdictions (and provide the benefit of military engagement with the United States) and has been used to good effect against North Korean vessels.

The Bush administration has also taken a bold and constructive step

8. *Onion,* March 26, 2003 (Issue 39, no. 11).

to supplant the Kyoto approach to global warming with a consortium of Australia, China, and other states. The United States has been vilified since Kyoto's inception in 1997 for not acceding to the treaty; the wonder is that we allowed the negative characterization to continue for so long without offering attractive alternatives that meet our needs. The Australia Group includes high–greenhouse gas emitters (the United States and Australia) and developing economies (China) and is exploring ways to use market mechanisms to improve on the Kyoto approach. If it succeeds, the Australia Group will provide a better alternative that Kyoto signatories can turn to. It will also give a precedent for multilateral cooperation, started by a core group and then expanded to broad participation, rather than making universal participation the starting point.

The three strategies have different consequences and require enormous investments of creativity, diplomacy, and political attention to supplant the default of continuing to work through institutions that are badly positioned for an international order dominated by our power. However, we need a better approach than the current alliance relationships and institutional structures are producing. Our strategic challenge in the time of our hegemony is burden sharing. We need to find ways to encourage and enable others to solve problems, and for the foreseeable future that means working through institutions. To adapt those institutions, we need to offer attractive alternatives and persuade other states that the changes are in their interest.

If we are looking at another American century because of our power, it is in our interest to invest in a web of institutions and relationships that allow us over time to shift the management of more problems into their care. The problems still may not end up solved in ways we would have chosen if we'd led the effort, but orchestrating the effort of others rather than doing it ourselves increases our ability to manage problems.

Encouraging leadership in others, creating new institutions to confront specific problems, encouraging institutions to compete for responsibilities, helping other countries solve the problems at the top of their agendas in order to buy their commitment to addressing our concerns, approaching strategic communications as a way to show our understanding of the world and our values rather than to convey our policies—they all contribute to improving the ways we have for shaping the international order and softening anti-American attitudes over time.

Realigning alliances and institutions to better fit the circumstances of an international order in which the United States is dominant does not require finding solutions to Einstein's three unsolved equations; it takes what any baseball fan would recognize as a small-ball approach to foreign policy: modest efforts where opportunities present themselves, aimed at achieving specific objectives, with advantages for countries willing to take a leadership role, giving precedents for a very different set of relations better tailored to the work at hand. These new relations won't always produce the results we want, but they will certainly shield us against overreach or isolation better than the existing institutional architecture does. For even if it were true that only the United States could solve problems in the present, this is no argument for perpetuating that singularity. If it is in our interest to have others share the burden of maintaining international peace and security, it is in our interest to help them do so—the alternative is a more chaotic international order with the rising costs to America of maintaining it.

CHAPTER 6

Four Choices for
the Next President

★   ★   ★

This has been a book about American power in a changing international order. It has sought to analyze why the United States has been so successful at this juncture of globalization, and whether our advantages are enduring or transitory. It concludes that the United States has succeeded internationally for reasons deeply rooted in the political culture of the country: the tolerance of risk and failure, the veneration of individual initiative, the encouragement of immigration, fewer constraints on social and economic mobility than most other countries, and—critically—a malleable, absorptive definition of itself. These fundamental precepts make American power self-rejuvenating in ways other societies cannot easily match. Moreover, globalization is reinforcing these advantages.

The fear of many anti-globalization activists that American practices will gain wider acceptance as individuals have greater choice seems justified. The restlessness for improvement and accessibility of culture that characterize American society may be decried as lowest common denominators, but there is no denying the successful formulas that make Disneyland and Hollywood movies and the iPod desirable commodities. As individuals are freed up from localized constraints (which is the fundamental dynamic of globalization), the self-interested choices they appear to portend a reinforcement of American power. If the rules of the international order continue to permit competition, the twentieth century may be seen as the harbinger rather than the zenith of American power, with the twenty-first century embodying American principles and practices throughout much of the international order.

All of which is not to say that the United States is an ideal hegemon, that it faces no grave domestic problems, or that it could not be confronted by ruinous challenges that collapse our power and the international order as we have known it. But the means of sustaining American power are largely in our own hands: the pervasiveness of American power hinges on the continued ability of the United States to remain adaptive and to create a vision of the international order that other states and organizations want to participate in. American hegemony has been affordable because its attractiveness has created a dynamic of voluntary accession that kept costs down and distributed them among the beneficiaries of the order.

In coming to terms with recent challenges, mainly the rise of terrorism and the desire by other states for international regimes that constrain U.S. behavior, we have not acquitted ourselves with notable congeniality. This has led many commentators to portend the demise of American power, including Paul Kennedy, Charles Kupchan, and Cullen Murphy. Adam Gopnik, writing in the *New Yorker,* sees reduced friction among transatlantic allies because America is irrelevant to European calculations.[1] This is an intellectually interesting concept but absurdly overstated. If it were true, the European Central Bank would not be pumping liquidity into global markets to ward off contagion from the subprime mortgage problems in the United States.

But likability is only one element of power. It is satisfying in its own right and its emollience reduces the cost of enforcement, surely. However, the cure for anti-Americanism will be reconstituting appreciation for the mutually beneficial nature of American power among other states. The dichotomy of hard power versus soft power is a false choice: a country as powerful as the United States needs to use both; moreover, it does use both, and reasonably well.

The United States does face several paradigm-defining choices, however. The Bush administration has made its choices and has little trade space to revisit them, with so little time remaining in its tenure. The next president will not exactly have a tabula rasa, but she or he will be able to make four fundamental choices that will either strengthen or weaken

1. Paul Kennedy, *Preparing For the Twenty First Century* (Vintage Books, 1993); Charles Kupchan, *Power in Transition* (Tokyo, Japan: United Nations University Press); Cullen Murphy, *Are We Rome?* (New York: Houghton Mifflin, 2007); Adam Gopnik, "The Human Bomb," (*New Yorker,* Aug. 27, 2007).

American power and have precedent-setting effects in the international order:

1. What should we do about the national debt?
2. Do we have to change the world?
3. How should we leave Iraq?
4. How should we structure and fund national security?

If these questions are not addressed as conscious choices, the president will nonetheless be defined by their answers. He or she will simply have forgone the ability to craft coherent approaches to the problems and will be driven by events, budgets, and other incremental forcing functions.

Debtor Nation

There are many good reasons for states to incur national debt, even of substantial magnitude, including the need for short-term capital to finance otherwise unaffordable wars or for spreading the long-term cost of major infrastructure projects. Long-term projects of staggering cost could include building an intercontinental fast train system connecting principal transport hubs, webbing the country with free wireless networks to reduce the income-based technology gap, initiating a step-change advance in learning, or setting up worker education programs to create skills at pivotal points of economic transition. We are not doing any of these things, although perhaps we should be.

We are, nonetheless, the largest debtor nation of the international order. Despite a $13 trillion economy and median household income of $46,000, our government is running $1.5 billion behind cash receipts in paying its bills every single day.[2] This is an unconscionable burden to impose on future taxpayers, and the most important strategic vulnerability of American power. Total federal debt is $9 trillion, which accords to about $30,000 for every single person in the country.

It is possible to overstate the fragility that U.S. debt represents. The

2. U.S. National Debt Clock, as of September 11, 2007, www.brillig.com/debt_clock; median household income is from the Census Bureau, August 29, 2006, http://www.whitehouse.gov/fsbr/income.html.

holders of debt could not make a run on the banks without seriously damaging the value of their own holdings, because sellers need buyers that would be frightened off if a purge of dollar holdings were suspected. In the extreme scenario of a stampede, the dollar still being the main reserve currency, major holders would probably intervene to preserve its value, as they did after the 9/11 attacks. Black hat sellers would probably be quarantined rather than the dollar spiraling downward. Even an attempt to collapse the value of the dollar would create systemic repercussions damaging to every stakeholder in the international economy, and would very likely be detected early and prevented by central banks and investment firms.

The great risk of the United States being so deeply mortgaged is not a short-term punitive strike on the dollar, but a long-term erosion of confidence in the United States as the rule setter of the global order and therefore of the dollar as the reserve currency. The United States gains enormous benefit from the long-standing perception of dollar holdings as stable value over time. That value derives from two sources: the productivity of the American economy, which historically grows at faster rates than other low-risk economies; and the independence and sound judgment of the Federal Reserve in managing inflation and the systemic health of the banking system.

If confidence in the dollar were to weaken, inflation would be a much more important problem for macroeconomic management, the cost of borrowing would increase to the U.S. government, our ability to influence the economic choices of other major stakeholders in the order would decrease, and the malaise of consumer pessimism inhibiting consumption would ensure a profound economic slump of perhaps long duration. The flip side of the attractiveness of dollar holdings to governments and large institutional investors is that the United States could eventually be hemmed in by their concerns about our economic choices, if our debt grows large enough and their holdings substantial enough. Since Chinese government and quasi-government dollar holdings now amount to $573 billion, we may be approaching the pivot point at which one holder's stake is large enough to dictate terms, limiting our freedom of action.

The most frustrating element of U.S. vulnerability due to indebtedness is that we have so little to show for it. The achievements of securing the international order were established without the edifice of debt that we now are pressed up against. No challenger arising has forced us into a costly arms race. No great physical monuments have been bought or systems of long-term improvement put into place that justify the risk associated with a $9 trillion debit column. Our indebtedness results from simple poor husbandry, a self-indulgence of living beyond our means and not making cost-effective choices.

There is no investment the U.S. government could make, or capability it could acquire, that would add as much to American power and to a stable, prosperous international order as would paying down our national debt. Breaking the cycle of deficit spending will grow harder, not easier, as the severity of reduction grows commensurate with the size of the debt. We now face no catastrophic challenge that justifies an unbalanced budget or perpetuating this enormous debt. We simply lack the political will to pay it off. Political leaders are averting their eyes from their responsibility to keep the country on a stable footing economically. The U.S. government should be ashamed not to have accomplished what Putin's Russian government has in the past five years in paying off its debt.

Reducing our debt is the simplest and most difficult challenge facing the country. Trade-offs will be politically unpopular and painful. And yet, this window of prosperity and dominance in the international order is the best time to accept near-term sacrifice and risk to ensure long-term well-being. If we cannot do it now, we cannot do it, and we will have sown the seeds of our own demise as the only country with the ability to shape the international order to its preferences.

Wilsonian Visions

Coming into office in 2001, the Bush administration focused national security on maintaining positive relations among the great powers of the international order. They were reflexively hesitant about using American power to achieve complicated political effects elsewhere. Condoleezza Rice exemplified the feel of the administration as it took office, saying "we don't need to have the 82nd Airborne escorting kids to kindergarten" and writing that the American military "is not a civilian police force. It is not a political referee. And it is most certainly not designed to build a civilian society."[3]

The September 11 attacks effected a sea change in administration attitudes about involvement in countries failing the challenge of adaptation. Before the attacks, the Bush administration considered it adequate to exclude from our attention states that were opting out of the emerging order, instead focusing on creating a strong central core of powerful and successful globalized partners. There was an understandable belief that the states that were opting out of the benefits of globalization or were incapable of governing to the advantage of their publics would remain ineffectual. This perhaps underestimated the force of resentment from states that chose self-defeating paths or were attempting to shield their societies from the changes globalization wrought.

After September 11, the stable, self-interested choices of the great powers appeared comfortably predictable in comparison with the dangers posed by failing states or with states that rejected the benefits of positive-sum globalization. The administration embraced a philosophy that the United States could not be safe unless we created the world in our image—a world of inalienable individual rights respected by representative governments and protected by law. Not only did the administration acknowledge threats from the periphery of unsuccessful states but democracy was seen as the cure for terrorism.

To use Walter Russell Mead's lexicography, the administration moved from being mainly Jacksonian to Wilsonian: from hesitance about international activism in the service of grand ideals to believing that our security was inextricably linked to other countries' adopting at least the central tenets of our formula for success.[4]

The political philosophy of stamping out terrorism where it is taking root by expanding political freedom there has strong echoes of Edmund Burke in his speeches on conciliation with America: "freedom and not servitude is the cure of anarchy; as religion, and not atheism, is the true

3. Condoleezza Rice, cited in "The Hobbled Hegemon," *Economist,* July 27, 2007. The passage on military missions is from "Campaign 2000: Promoting the National Interest," *Foreign Affairs* (January/February 2000): p. 53.
4. Mead, *Special Providence.*

remedy for superstition."[5] Fundamental to this approach is the belief that the causes of terrorism against the United States are local, a reflection of frustration with the lack of opportunity and ability to create political change in that society. Terrorist acts against the United States are thus symbolic destruction because we represent the forces of change that the attackers want to shield their own societies from experiencing, but attacks will occur here unless we fix the problem where it grows.

The next president should think carefully about whether these precepts are true. Is terrorism a threat of the magnitude to justify this level of effort by the United States? Do we need to change the world to be safe ourselves? Is fostering change in countries where terrorism is burgeoning likely to defang terrorism or further fuel its virulence?

The magnitude of the threat. The argument against terrorism as a major threat has two parts: first, that because no catastrophic attacks have occurred in the United States since 9/11, the threat may not be as grave as initial reactions assumed; and second, that Al Qaeda is an aberration rather than the norm of a new genre of international terrorism. In the six years since the 9/11 attacks, the U.S. government has increased the baseline defense budget by 62 percent, even before the direct costs of the Iraq War (covered in the defense supplemental spending bill) are factored in.[6] The Congressional Budget Office estimates current Iraq War costs to be $2 billion a week; several independent assessments estimate it at $1.2 trillion so far.[7] These figures should raise questions about the cost-effectiveness and sustainability of our strategy for combating terrorism.

Concern about terrorism also shifted the U.S. agenda toward involvement in Pakistan, Afghanistan, and Iraq, with opportunity costs in other relationships, such as those with Russia and Mexico, that had been central to the administration's vision of cementing great power relations

5. Burke, Second Speech on Conciliation with America. The difference with Burke in a terrorism analogy, however, is that Britain and America were one political and cultural society; when Al Qaeda attacked the United States, it was attacking "the other," not its own.

6. Office of Management and Budget, "The President's 2008 Budget," http://www.white house/gov/omb/budget/fy2008/defense.htm.

7. Brian Bender, "Cost of Iraq War," *Boston Globe,* September 28, 2006. For exploration of cost estimates, see David Leonhardt, "What $1.2 Trillion Can Buy," *New York Times,* January 17, 2007.

and solving near concerns like uncontrolled immigration. From the perspective of imposing strategic effect, Al Qaeda's attacks on the United States created an enormous perturbation, diverting resources and effort in epic proportion from other priorities.

However, it would be irresponsible to conclude that because there have been no other successful attacks, Al Qaeda is not attempting them. The evidence points overwhelmingly in the opposite direction: that despite operating with the bulk of American military and intelligence effort against them, Al Qaeda continues to plan and attempt to carry out sensationally devastating attacks. There is nothing in their statements or activities that suggests Al Qaeda is content with damage already achieved or moderating its goals. The Bin Laden tape from September 10, 2007, reaffirms that even major changes in U.S. policy, such as completely withdrawing the U.S. military and diplomatic presence in the Middle East, are not enough to appease Al Qaeda aspirations.[8]

Al Qaeda or terrorism in general? At a minimum, the United States has an Al Qaeda threat that must be contended with. A related inquiry is whether we have a generalized terrorism problem or specifically an Al Qaeda problem. No other terrorist groups have emerged to rival Al Qaeda in scope or danger or effectiveness. Might the aperture of the "global war on terror" be narrowed solely to Al Qaeda, excluding other terrorist movements from our scope of action? This is in many ways a more difficult question. It is clear that terrorist groups share tactics and in some instances training and funding; it is less clear that there is a global network of terrorists with shared goals. Most terrorist acts seem to have local political motivations: increasing the cost to Israel of holding territory in the West Bank or southern Lebanon, frightening Western tourists from Bali, preventing popular support for political solutions to the status of Northern Ireland, increasing Spanish willingness to allow Basque independence, blowing up a government building in Oklahoma in a convoluted antigovernment protest. Even the 2004 train attacks in Spain seemed to have the purpose of peeling Spain away from the Iraq coalition, rather than a more general "destroy the West" aim.

8. In the September 10 tape, Osama Bin Laden states that conversion to Islam is the only means by which the United States could end Al Qaeda attacks.

If most terrorism has localized aims, it could be argued that treating the problems separately, with an eye to political solutions that isolate forces of violence, and solving political issues by peaceful means might be more productive approaches than combating all terrorist groups as though they were Al Qaeda.

To further the argument for combating Al Qaeda rather than all terrorism, if one accepts that most terrorism is localized in its political intent, the United States would need to become very involved in the local political problems to help develop solutions. Even aligning ourselves against any party that chooses violence against civilians requires us to take sides. Becoming a party to the conflict, even in this limited way, could increase the risk of terrorist acts against the United States, as terrorist methods with longer reach are shared in even a loose network of terrorist organizations. Perhaps by not getting involved in other societies' struggles, coupled with better port and border security in the United States and a continued press on Al Qaeda, the United States would be more secure?

There are two problems with adopting such a narrow approach to combating terrorism. First, it assumes that others will dedicate effort to helping us solve our problem although we are unwilling to help them solve the problems they are most concerned about (localized terrorist groups) or limit our engagement to punitive means. Second, it ignores the milieu in which Al Qaeda and other terrorist groups exist. They may communicate and pass money virtually, but they still live and act in physical space. States and individuals still have to make choices about whether to permit them transit and assistance or to share information and take common action against the terrorist groups.

The Bush administration's choice after the 9/11 attacks to hold states accountable for activity that emanates from within their borders was a major step forward in extending deterrence into the realm of terrorism. Globalization may have eroded some elements of state sovereignty, but states are still the possessors and guardians of territory. U.S. strategy situates the accountability for activity occurring in their realms at the level of governments, which are more easily influenced than terrorist groups because they have a wider range of interests that can be cajoled and coerced. If the United States takes no interest in the political troubles of states bedeviled by terrorism, as a practical matter we are much less likely to gain those states' assistance with our own. Moreover, the states in which terrorism tends to take root are those states with the least ability for governance, and it would seem to doubly penalize them if we did choose not to help build the means of managing their political problems.

Real unilateralism. Another way of asking the question about whether we need a Wilsonian strategy is to ask whether the United States can be safe and prosperous in a squalid international environment. It is a bedrock assertion of the 2002 National Security Strategy that the United States could not remain an open and vibrant society only playing defense in the fight against terrorism. This is probably true, but merits careful examination. Since the U.S. economy is one of the most integrated with the rest of the world, it would stand to reason that there would be a penalty in reduced commerce, physical and virtual. But, as somewhat increased airport and seaport security has demonstrated in a more restrictive post-9/11 environment, the penalties are mostly in the hassle and delay of delivery time, not in the completion of delivery. Since the U.S. market remains so lucrative (we manufacture few of our own consumer goods) and innovative, it remains well worth the effort for foreign businesses to invest and trade here. New opportunities have also sprung up where impediments destroyed previous businesses.

The all-important issue of immigration might likewise cut both ways: fewer talented people may choose to come to the United States or be able to gain visas for legal entry if we pull up our drawbridges to the rest of the world. On the other hand, if the rest of the world grows more dangerous and unpredictable, it could increase the desire of the most talented people to come to the safe harbor of the United States.

As a question of prosperity, the United States could most likely manage the transition to a more dangerous international order. The transition could even be profitable, if investors accorded a significant differential to U.S. holdings because they were judged more secure. Our economy would probably become more volatile, though, susceptible to wider swings in investor concerns about the security of assets outside the United States. Since market volatility tends to raise the price of borrowing, inhibit some kinds of long-term investment, and generally reduce consumer confidence, such volatility would very likely be damaging both to the United States and the global economy.

The question of a separate peace, in which the United States cares less and risks less to lay a systemic foundation in which other states also enjoy peace, seems likewise ill-advised. Americans may insist that Wilsonian crusades are underpinned by Jacksonian assessments of national interest, and periodically tire of policing the international order, but we repeatedly go in for making the world a better place. The foreboding that would accompany secession from the battle against terrorists broadly would cast a long pall over who we are as an optimistic political culture. From a perusal of presidential candidates' pronouncements, it also seems not to be where they believe American attitudes are headed: every major candidate advocates continuing to prosecute the war on terror.

Leaving Iraq

Whoever the next American president is, she or he probably will decide when the United States withdraws its troops from Iraq. Absent congressional insistence, it is almost impossible to envision President Bush supervising the denouement of this war, because of the alarming aftermath were it disengaged soon. Even if Congress were to legislate an end to U.S. military deployments in Iraq, the president might be willing to run out the clock of his administration with a pocket veto, reprogramming existing funds, or court challenge of congressional authority to force withdrawal of troops from combat in wartime.

Americans have had a reassuringly vibrant debate about Iraq, as befits a democracy at war. The media has kept the war in the center of national attention, the 2004 presidential race hinged on the issue, Congress has regained its balance and is legislating oversight of executive decisions, candidates for president in 2008 are all being vetted by their views on Iraq. Moreover, the debate has accurately crystallized the fundamental issue: whether Iraqi leaders are making enough political progress on the hard decisions that will stabilize their country to merit our continued effort on their behalf. Few outside the White House believe we are fully succeeding in Iraq, yet there remains a reservoir of appreciation that it is very much in American interests to succeed, and some optimism that the administration's most recent approach may yet do so. That optimism will have either been proven or extinguished before President Bush's term concludes.

Success or failure in Iraq hinges crucially on the ability and willingness of Iraq's political leaders to make brave choices. They have done a poor job so far. The choices will unquestionably be made more difficult, and the temptations of Al Qaeda and neighboring states to capitalize on Iraq's fractures will dramatically increase, without the stabilizing presence of American military forces. The next president will have the latitude to decide whether to continue to prosecute the war in Iraq. The new presidency will not be defined by the choice of going to war, but it could well be defined by how the new president ends it.

Maximal harm. The costliest way, of course, would be to withdraw precipitously, amid cries of abandonment by Iraqi political leaders, leaving a vacuum into which Al Qaeda, Iran, Syria, and other parties unconcerned with Iraq's well-being descend. In historically comparable cases, withdrawal of the guarantor (whether colonial power or other external actor) collapses the political center. People and political factions that had cooperated in governance and security are killed or politically neutralized, and threats of violence determine the political space making, which drives communal activity to extremes of the political spectrum.

All estimates of Iraqi security forces converge on two points: (1) that the Iraqi army is making slow but sure progress toward a force with numbers adequate to Iraq's needs and toward the ability to conduct autonomous military operations against Al Qaeda and other violent forces in the country; and (2) the Iraqi police have been badly infiltrated by the Mahdi army, Iranian operatives, and other factional forces.[9] There is no reason to believe that in the coming two years the Iraqi police will be a force for anything but sectarian retributive attacks against the populations they are supposed to be protecting. This means that if U.S. forces were to withdraw, either the Iraqi police would brutalize Iraqis with

9. The Iraq Survey Group, the Government Accountability Office, and General Petraeus' September 2007 assessment all make this point. For a more detailed assessment, see Anthony H. Cordesman, *Iraq Force Development: Conditions for Success, Consequences of Failure* (Center for Strategic and International Studies, September 2007).

impunity, or the Iraqi military would turn against the police force—in effect, taking military control of the country's internal security.

Besides the calamitous effects on Iraq itself, a rapid withdrawal from Iraq would be extraordinarily damaging to American credibility. It is difficult to imagine that any country would now choose a "freedom agenda" of the kind envisioned early on as a chain reaction effect of the war in Iraq; the potential for crippling violence and political fractiousness and exposure to regional enemies would loom too large. Managing the Iraq War badly has strengthened the hand of repressive governments who can point to the Pandora's box of violent upheaval in Iraq to justify continued control. It has also inhibited democratic forces from accepting U.S. assistance.

The management of the Iraq War has also called American commitment and competence into question among allies and enemies both. Many countries that contributed forces to the Iraq coalition believed our success would burnish their reputations as well, and have found the inverse also holds true. They would also have some reason to doubt whether our efforts in their defense might be damaging to their political, economic, and military objectives. Iraq will almost certainly provoke allies like South Korea to want greater control over American efforts where their countries are concerned, trusting our independent actions less.

Withdrawal from Iraq also has potentially titanic effects on regional stability in the Middle East. The Saudi condemnation of the United States for facilitating a "Shi'ia rise" is tiresome, as the Saudi government has done little to help Iraqis in tamping down sectarian violence or even interdicting the flow of fighters entering Iraq across the Saudi border. Moreover, the Saudi preference for continued Sunni dominance of a majority Shi'ia Iraqi public is questionable. Finally, the rise of Iran is not simply a function of the difficulties Iraq is experiencing: Iran may be shrewdly capitalizing on Iraq's misfortune, but there are many untapped means available to the Saudi government and other neighbors to constrain Iran's influence.

Turkey's restraint in Iraq—as diaphanously thin as it sometimes has been since 2003—has been engendered by U.S. involvement. Several Turkish government objectives have not been delivered by the United States, such as shutting down Mujahedin-e Khalq (MEK) operations in northern Iraq and restoring cross-border trade, but Turkey has been understandably reticent to confront U.S. forces. Were the United States to withdraw, it is difficult to envision Turkey not crossing into Iraq to control MEK activity, even if it restrained itself from the broader objective of preventing the emergence of a Kurdish state. The Kurdish nightmare scenario is even plausible in the instance of a rapid United States withdrawal: Iran, Syria, and Turkey scrambling for conquest of the Kurdish areas of Iraq to prevent an autonomous Kurdistan whose map overlay would have claims in each of their territories.

Minimal harm. The faster and more recklessly the United States withdraws from Iraq, the greater the cost in credibility will be. A successful program for withdrawal of U.S. forces from Iraq would, at the least, require

- gradual reductions calibrated to reduce ensuing violence;
- programs to neutralize and then professionalize the Iraqi police;
- collaboration with the Iraqi government on the timeline and trajectory of transferring responsibility;
- commitment by other states to take up the training and equipping of Iraqi security forces that the United States will leave off doing;
- accommodating of the interests and cajoling of positive engagement by regional powers;
- providing economic incentives for continued cohesion of Iraq's sectarian communities;
- hedging against bad outcomes as they begin to emerge.

None of the withdrawal programs outlined by the Iraq Survey Group, Democratic presidential candidates, and other advocates of ending U.S. combat operations yet meet this standard.

The lessons states learn from Iraq will not all be enthusing to enemies and discomforting to allies of the United States. That we have continued to fight in Iraq longer than we contested World War II, and without notable victories to anchor public sentiment in favor of the war, is remarkable and may actually counterbalance some of the damage to U.S. credibility. The United States did attack a country believed to possess weapons of mass destruction, with the expectation it could already have nuclear weapons and would use them if they did. Public expectation was gauged to a rapid and low-cost victory that has not materialized: $1.2 trillion dollars and 3,774 Americans killed in action is much more than Americans expected to risk in order to achieve WMD control and regime change in Iraq.[10] It is less surprising that public support for the war has eroded than that the president still has substantial latitude to continue the war.

The army, in particular, has been strained, and required to make rapid and difficult adjustments as the nature of the war changed. But it has done well, demonstrating the seriousness and innovation that characterize transformation.

It is also surprising that the economic cost of the war has had so little negative effect. It speaks to the strength of the American economy that it could sustain the cost of the war with 5 percent growth and only 4 percent unemployment.

The data are also mixed on the severity of the blow Iraq has struck to American power. Iran appears resurgent from the concerns that animated its 2003 offer of broad cooperation with the United States; Saudi Arabia is making cautious moves to a leadership role on Palestinian and regional security issues; Egypt, Syria, and other states have retrenched against democratization. While disturbing, these are not uniformly bad developments; Saudi activism in particular is long overdue and could lead to positive outcomes, even if different from what the United States envisioned.

One should also be careful not to oversubscribe the effect: Iran's regional activism and gallop toward nuclear capability were underway, and Egypt was distorting prospects for peaceful post-Mubarak governance, long before U.S. difficulties in Iraq. It is even possible that Libya's denunciation of its weapons ambitions had more to do with economic malaise than concern about American intervention. In the most trying time of U.S. involvement in Iraq, North Korea finally struck a nuclear freeze deal that it is carrying out, something previous American governments had been unsuccessful in achieving. As the next president chooses how to wind up U.S. involvement in Iraq, reinforcing the strengths shown by the United States throughout the years of the Iraq War will have an important effect on how long a shadow our difficulties in Iraq cast.

---

10. Fatality figure as of September 11, 2007, http://www.icasualties.org/oif/BY_DOD.aspx.

National Security: Structure and Resourcing

The American strategy for national security in the age of combating terrorism is a complicated undertaking, attempting as it does the creation of sophisticated political, economic, and social effects. We have chosen not simply to destroy what threatens us but to help in the creation of positive alternatives, and to spend our money fostering civil society and strengthening the ability for governance in places doing the least well at those challenges. The snarky triumphalist maxim that "superpowers don't do windows" has been proven untrue.[11] The United States does windows—quite literally, with U.S. forces in Iraq spending Commander's Emergency Response Funds to replace school windows—because constraining our engagement to simply punitive involvement raises the cost to us of ensuring an international order that fosters our interests.

The strategy is both elegant and virtuous. The problem with the strategy is that we are incapable of truly carrying it out. Our government is poorly organized for orchestrating a delicate minuet of activity at varying speeds and using a multiplicity of tools under the control of different departments that have effects with widely varying timeframes and the assessment of whose success requires specialized and rarified knowledge. We are a government of amateurs, organized by founders (both in the original sense and in reference to the architects of the 1947 National Security Act) who were manifestly concerned about the concentration of power, and funded by a process that trades speed and agility for breadth of supervision.

It is important to separate the challenges of effective policy making from effective policy execution. The divisions within the U.S. government, aligned as they are by departments with the means and responsibilities of carrying out different government activities, actually suit the task of policy making extremely well. James Madison himself might clap his small hands in delight at the design of a system in which interests are known and balanced against each other. The National Security Council has the president's mandate and seeks to preserve it against policies that would damage or distract attention from his priorities. The State Department holds precedence on issues of diplomatic value, the Defense

11. John Hillen, "Superpowers Don't Do Windows," *Orbis* 41, no. 2 (Spring 1997): pp. 241–57.

Department on using force, the Treasury Department on economic effect, the Justice Department on domestic legal ramifications, the Commerce Department on business competitiveness. The system generally produces internal debate and differing perspectives sufficient to test the soundness and costs of policy in development.

So the problem is not policy formation but policy execution: the carrying out of agreed functions by departments of the executive branch, with funding and legal boundaries provided by the Congress. If the U.S. government cannot be machinated to carry out strategies with concordant political, economic, and military elements, three alternatives are before us: the continuing risk of suboptimal performance in executing a sensible strategy, lowering our sights to a simpler set of objectives that the current system can more reliably produce, or restructuring the interagency system to increase the prospect of suitable outcomes. As the first two are both self-explanatory and inadequate, debate on whether and how to restructure the interagency for better policy execution has become the focus of attention.

The critics of the Bush administration often claim that with better management the interagency system has worked fine in the past. It is true that at earlier points in time the interagency system has performed better than at present and has achieved its stated objectives. It is also true that previous administrations have almost always struggled with effective right hand–left hand coordination of the means of national power. The problem is endemic, not specific to the Bush administration. Moreover, contemporary objectives are distinct in two crucial ways: first, the strategy has more complex and multivariate elements than previous strategies; and second, the time window has dramatically narrowed for government action before public scrutiny. In short, the standard has gone up, but the structure and practices of interagency coordination have not improved commensurate with the need.[12]

The great difficulty in coordinating the political, economic, and military aspects of the president's strategy has spawned numerous think tank efforts to redesign the interagency process. The Clinton administration

12. The Project on National Security Reform is exploring many facets of how to improve interagency coordination, including structure, processes, funding, and personnel needs. The project aims to advise Congress and the executive branch on ways to improve performance by 2008. See www.pnsr.org.

acknowledged the problem, issuing Presidential Directive 56. Most reviews recommend the creation of new offices in the National Security Council to better coordinate stability operations (the government term for military forces operating in complex political environments, ostensibly with coordinating political and economic elements).[13] This answer fails to sight the horizon line of the problems, which are much bigger than an office within the National Security Council's staff could possibly take control of. It creates enormous reporting and coordination requirements without affecting departmental choices at the highest levels. At best, it can serve to identify for senior policymakers the lower-level failures of coordination.

The two central problems plaguing the interagency process are resourcing and responsibility. The resourcing problem is elemental: with a $465 billion defense budget and a $60 billion diplomatic and foreign aid budget, we are dramatically underresourced on the non-military side of the equation. Six thousand foreign service officers and a culture that is not aligned to the dangerous expeditionary work match up poorly with the demands in the president's strategy for building stable democracies. It cannot produce a political development that will keep pace with the military activity. And yet we continue to fund the piece of the puzzle at which we perform best—military operations—without strengthening the elements at which our performance is worst: the civilian political and economic components. Unless we dramatically increase capacity in the civilian departments, our military will continue to be pushed into development work, diplomatic counsel, engagement with religious leaders, the establishment of local political structures, the provision of essential services like electricity, and many other tasks for which it is neither trained nor by which we send the right signal of American intentions.

The resource imbalance is on the order of $80 billion dollars a year. Hiring and training the diplomats, development assistance experts, justice system advisors, infrastructure engineers, police trainers, economists, translators, and other civilian constituents that could move

13. See Michele Flournoy, *Goldwater Nichols* (Washington, D.C.: Center for Strategic and International Studies, 2004).

into a country in sufficient numbers to build near-term stability and longer-term institutional capability is an expensive proposition.

Then there is the cost of changing the State Department's culture. Except in language training, diplomats are not given adequate opportunities for professional education comparable with the gates built into military careers. The size of the diplomatic corps doesn't allow for it, the personnel system doesn't give incentives for it, and as a result, the profession does not develop a shared core of knowledge and values that can be called into alignment with the country's changing needs. It is absolutely shameful that the State Department took so long to man the U.S. embassy in Iraq, but diplomats are understandably concerned about their safety. Political-military Action Teams were created in both Afghanistan and Iraq to marry military security with diplomatic activity, which seems a sensible solution. However, nearly one-third of the State Department's one hundred slots have now been assigned to the Defense Department because the State Department is unable to staff them, even though Iraq is the president's top foreign policy priority. Our foreign service has a cultural problem we need to address if even trebling the service's funding is to create the strong political presence necessary for international operations that have integral political and military objectives.

Not only are the proportions of the budget poorly aligned with the capabilities needed but the process of making and carrying out policy reinforces departmental loyalties rather than presidential priorities. Departments defend their institutional prerogatives in the policy making process and often choose policies that reduce their responsibilities rather than increase the likelihood of success. Even the term "interagency process" suggests the combination of independent elements rather than an inner-government, executive branch approach. Here the Goldwater-Nichols precedent of Defense Department reform may have salience.[14]

The 1986 reforms forced greater cooperation among the military services, and separated the functions of recruiting, training, and equipping the force from its use in combat. Both of these elements have parallels

14. I have explored this idea jointly with Bruce Berkowitz in "National Security: A Better Approach," *Hoover Digest,* no. 4 (Stanford, CA: Hoover Institution Press, 2005).

in the interagency policy process. Before the Goldwater-Nichols legislation, military departments were nearly autonomous, developing their own equipment and war plans, with no incentive for capitalizing on each others' expertise to develop a common approach. Goldwater-Nichols personnel policies that required general officers to have experience outside their service, professional military education that brought talented officers into joint environments, and senior jobs that critically affected service equities opened to competition from other services all contributed to the military departments' giving their officers broader experience. Later reforms extending the requirement for the joint evaluation of weapons and competition for mission areas have extended the principle further. Executive direction or congressional legislation that required senior executives in the Departments of State, Treasury, Defense, Justice, and Homeland Security to have similar broadening would make for better functioning and inherently interagency approaches, although it is difficult to see how that would be imposed on political appointees.

Perhaps the most important Goldwater-Nichols reforms were those that shifted the focus of warfighting from inputs to results. When the service chiefs were only responsible for their piece of the war, accountability was difficult to establish, and their principal loyalty was producing service combat power. With the creation of Combatant Command posts, the scope of activity for service chiefs was narrowed to being force providers. Combatant commanders had the responsibility affixed to them to take those forces and produce results. Combatant commanders develop war plans incorporating all kinds of military power and command the force in combat. The separation of responsibilities institutionalizes the near- and long-term responsibilities and provides them advocates in the process, while also making the line of authority clear.

There is no position that parallels combatant commanders in the executive branch. Policy making and execution are the responsibility of the equivalents of service chiefs, the cabinet secretaries. There is no one the president can charge with developing the plans that integrate political, economic, and military means and then carrying out those plans. The national security advisor lacks execution authority and is unlikely to get it absent submitting the president's personal staff to congressional confirmation (which would permit directing large amounts of congressionally appropriated money). Cabinet secretaries have execution authority but not the totality of means, which remains organized in other departments. Both the development of plans and their execution are collective responsibilities, with guidance and, in some administrations, direction from the National Security Advisor.

Unless cabinet secretaries are circumscribed to being force providers, we should not expect the executive branch to produce integrated strategies. Unless some civilian combatant commanders are appointed by the president, confirmed by Congress, given some influence over budget allocation, and authorized to develop and carry out policies, they will never be the peers of cabinet secretaries and therefore never be able to redirect focus from the departmental inputs to presidential priority outcomes. The system desperately needs such leaders with the authority and resources that will enable them to achieve results. The above are radical solutions, but responsibilities and authorities will not otherwise align to produce integrated strategies or the effective orchestration of the political, military, and economic elements of our national power.

The dysfunctional interagency process for executing policy has impeded American power more than any external foe. We must either ratchet back the degree of sophistication we plan for in the use of American power, or we must find ways to improve our performance—anything else dishonors the sacrifices made by those Americans contributing most and nearly ensures that the costs of achieving complicated effects (such as regime change) will be prohibitive.

One final thought: our government is surprisingly bad at many things that we as a society are incredibly good at, such as shaping attitudes, affecting outcomes we lack control over, creating incentives for cooperation, bringing the strengths of civil society to bear on problems, encouraging localized activity that cumulatively affects large issues. We have to get better as a government at harnessing our strengths if we are to make profitable use of the inherent advantages of American political culture.

Conclusion

American power is of a unique kind, converging as it does economic, military, diplomatic, linguistic, and cultural elements in a self-reinforcing mix. It has been a juggernaut of influence, advancing the globalization and Americanization of the international order. The dynamism of

American power has the potential to remain at the apogee of the international order, setting rules and ensuring the well-being of Americans for the foreseeable future. The greatest threats to American power are, in a strangely poetic way, our own choices about how to deal with indebtedness and about how to shape the behavior of other states into successful patterns as globalization advances, minimizing the damage of mistakes we have made in Iraq, and funding and organizing our government for effective policy execution. The means are within our grasp to ensure that our children have the prosperity and latitude of freedom we enjoyed in the American Century. We need only to face the changes bravely, as Americans traditionally have.

Measures of
State Power

★ ★ ★

Measures of State Power

ECONOMICS

Measure	US	Rest of World	UK	Japan	China	India	Russia	Germany	France	Iran
GDP ($)[1] (2005=actual)	12.417T	44.645T	2.199T	4.534T	2.234T (Hong Kong .178T)	.806T	.764T	2.795T	2.127T	.190T
GDP (Purchasing Power Parity—Estimated 2006)[2]	12.98T	65T	1.903T	4.220T	10T	4.042T	1.723T	2.585T	1.871T	.610T
GDP ($) (as Proportion of Actual Global GDP)[3]	27.81%	72.19% (other than US)	4.26%	9.45%	5.00%	1.81%	1.71%	6.26%	4.76%	0.43%
GDP Composition of Country by Sector[4]	agric. .9%, industry 20.4%, services 78.6% (06 est.)	agric. 4%, industry 32%, services 64% (04 est.)	agric. 1%, industry 25.6%, services 73.4% (06 est.)	agric. 1.6%, industry 25.3%, services 73.1% (06 est.)	agric. 11.9%, industry 48.1%, services 40% (06 est.)	agric. 19.9%, industry 19.3%, services 60.7% (05 est.)	agric. 5.3%, industry 36.6%, services 58.2% (06 est.)	agric. 0.9%, industry 29.1%, services 70% (06 est.)	agric. 2.2%, industry 20.6%, services 77.2% (06 est.)	agric. 11.2%, industry 41.7%, services 47.1% (06 est.)
Foreign Direct Investment, Net Inflows (BOP-US$) —World Bank[5]	109.754B (05) 133.163B (04) 63.961B (03)	974.283B (05) 731.125B (04) 639.739B (03)	158.800B (05) 77.949B (04) 27.612B (03)	3.214B (05) 7.805B (04) 6.238B (03)	79.127B (05) 54.937B (04) 47.076B (03)	6.598B (05) 5.474B (04), 4.585B (03)	15.151B (05) 15.444B (04) 7.958B (03)	32.034B (05) 15.104B (04) 27.724B (03)	70.686B (05) 38.709B (04) 43.068B (03)	.03B (05) .100B (04) .482B (03)
Foreign Direct Investment Inflows—2005 ($)—UNCTAD[6]	99B	916B	165B	2.8B	72B (with Hong Kong—108B)	not in top 20	15B	32B	63B	not in top 20
Workers' Remittances Received (US$–2005)[7]	2.924B	262.489B	6.722B	1.08B	22.492B	23.725B	3.117B	6.542B	12.742B	1.032B

Remittances Sent Abroad ($ –2004)[8]	39B (World Bank), 29.9B (GAO)	225.8B (World Bank)	Not Avail	Not Avail	Not Avail	Not Avail	Not Avail	5B (GAO)	4B (GAO)	Not Avail
Foreign Holders of U.S. Treasuries ($)—February 2007[9]	—	2,141B	119B	617.8B	416.2B Mainland / 57.4B Hong Kong	19.5B	Not Avail	47.9B	22.8B	110.8B (15 oil exporters including Iran)
Foreign Exchange Holdings of Each Country's Currency ($)—(2006, 4th Quarter & 1999, 4th Quarter)[10]	2,156M (06) / 979M (99)	5,028M (06) / 1,781M (99)	148M (06) / 40M (99)	106M (06) / 88M (99)	Not Avail	Not Avail	Not Avail	859M (06) / 247M (99) (Claims on Euros)	859M (06) / 247M (99) (Claims on Euros)	Not Avail
Business Bankruptcies / Total Bankruptcies[a,b] (# > 1)[11]	918,957 (out of 12,177,219) (7.5%)									
Time Required to Start a Business —2005 (days)[12]	5	47	18	31	48	71	33	24	8	47
FortuneGlobal 500 Companies (#) —2006[13]	170	500	39	70	20	6	5	35	38	0
# Foreign Companies that List on Stock Market (March 2007)[14]	NYSE 451 (out of 2249) NASDAQ 328 (out of 3120)		London 647 (out of 3245)	Tokyo 25 (out of 2413)	Shanghai 0 (out of 848) Hong Kong 9 (out of 1180) Shenzhen 0 (out of 601)	Bombay 0 (out of 4821) National Stock Exchange India 0 (out of 1126)	Not Avail	Deutsche Borse 100 (out of 755)	Euronext 246 (out of 1199)	Tehran 0 (out of 322)
Bank Branches per 100,000 People (2001–2004)[15]	30.9	9.8	18.3	10	1.3	6.3	2.2	49.4	43.2	8.4

Measures of State Power (*continued*)

Measure	US	Rest of World	UK	Japan	China	India	Russia	Germany	France	Iran
Charitable Giving (as a % of GDP) —2004[16]	1.67%		0.73%	NA	NA	NA	NA	0.22%	0.14%	NA
Highest Federal Marginal Tax Rate / On Income over $ / Corporate Tax Rate —2004[17]	35% / 319,100 / 35%		40% / 51,358 / 30%	37% / 167,395 / 30%	45% / 12,082 / 30% (Hong Kong 17% / 13,462 / 18%)	30% / 3,283 / 36%	13% / NA / 24%	45% / 65,224 / 25%	48% / 60,673 / 33%	35% / 1 25,345 / 25%

MILITARY

Measure	US	Rest of World	UK	Japan	China	India	Russia	Germany	France	Iran
Defense Spending ($) (2005, 2004, 2003)[18]	495.3B (05), 455.9B (04), 404.9B (03)	1,207B (05), 1,124B (04), 1,011B (03)	51.7B (05), 50.1B (04), 43.3B (03)	43.9B (05), 45.15B (04), 42.84B (03)	103.96 (05), 87.2B (04), 75.5B (03)	21.73B (05), 19.8B (04), 15.5B (03)	58B (05), 59.6B (04), 65.2B (03)	38.04B (05), 37.8B (04), 35.3B (03)	53.128B (05), 52.7B (04), 46.2B (03)	5.2B (05), 5.4B (04), 4.2B (03)
Defense Spending as % of GDP (2005, 2004, 2003)[18]	4.0 (05), 3.9 (04), 3.7 (03)	2.64 (05), 2.64 (04), 2.67 (03)	2.3 (05), 2.3 (04), 2.4 (03)	1 (05), 1 (04), 1 (03)	1.3 (05), 1.4 (04), 1.5 (03)	2.7 (05), 2.9 (04), 2.6 (03)	3.7 (05), 4.2 (04), 4.9 (03)	1.4 (05), 1.4 (04), 1.5 (03)	2.5 (05), 2.6 (04), 2.6 (03)	2.8 (05), 3.3 (04), 3.1 (03)

INTELLECTUAL

Measure	US	Rest of World	UK	Japan	China	India	Russia	Germany	France	Iran
Patents—# Application Filings Submitted in Country Office (Resident / Non-Resident/Total)[19]	202,776 / 182,866 / 390,733 (2005)		17,488 / 10,155 / 27,988 (2005)	359,382 / 59,118 / 427,078 (2005)	93,172 / 79,842 / 173,327 (2005)	6,795 / 10,287 / 17,466 (2004)	23,588 / 8,609 / 32,253 (2005)	47,537 / 11,855 / 60,222 (2005)	14,230 / 3,060 / 17,290 (2004)	360 (2004)
Nobel Prizes (%) / # Received[20]	36.4% / 258 (1901–2000), 55% (2001–2004)	63.60%	13% / 92 (1901–2000), 16% (2001–2004)	NA	NA	NA	2.5% / 18 (1901–2000)	10.5% / 74 (1901–2000)	6.9% / 49 (1901–2000)	NA

% of Foreign Students in a Country (2004)[21]	23.30%	100%	12.20%	4.80%		not in top 15	3.10%	10.60%	9.70%	not in top 15
Students from Abroad Studying in Given Country (2004)[22]	572,509	2,455,250	300,056	117,903	14,627 (Macao), 3,270 (Hong Kong)	7,738	75,786	260,314	237,587	1,791
Students Studying Abroad (2004) (top country going to, including USA if 2nd)[33]	41,181 (UK)	2,455,250 (USA)	23,542 (USA)	60,424 (USA)	343,126 (USA, Japan)/ 34,199 Hong Kong (Australia, USA)	123,559 (USA)	34,473 (Germany, USA)	56,410 (UK, USA)	53,350 (Belgium, USA)	17,524 (Germany, USA)
R&D Expenditure ($—PPP)[24]	265.2B (00)	729B (00)		98.4B (00)	48.9B (00)	20B (est.—00)			50.9B (00)	Non-US G-7 Countries— 242.1B (00)
Expenditures for R&D—% of GDP (1996–2004)[25]	2.60%	2.36%	1.89%	3.15%	1.31% (Hong Kong .6%)	0.85%	1.28%	2.50%	2.19%	Not Avail
Researchers in R&D (per million people) (1996–2004)[25]	4,484	Not Avail	2,706	5,287	663 (Hong Kong 1,564)	119	3,319	3,261	3,213	467
Scientific and Technical Journal Articles Published[25]	200,870	648,500	47,660	57,420	20,978 (Hong Kong 1,817)	11,076	15,846	43,623	31,317	995
Royalty and License Fees Receipts (millions $) 2004[25]	52,643	109,808	12,019	15,701	236 (Hong Kong 341)	25	227	5,103	5,070	Not Avail
Trademark Applications Filed (Residents / Non-residents) 2002[25]	181,693/ 30,944	1,316,564/ 604,897	51,399/ 17,135	100,645/ 16,827	321,034/ 57,597 (Hong Kong 5,903/ 14,543)	Not Avail	29,279/ 14,215	53,817/ 12,827	58,035/ 12,774	9,858/ 1,224

Measures of State Power (*continued*)

Measure	US	Rest of World	UK	Japan	China	India	Russia	Germany	France	Iran
Education (Literacy Rate—Age 15+ / % with Bachelor's Degree)[26]	99% (03) / 28% (06)	82% (05)	99% (03) / 15% (01)	99% (02)	90.9% (06)	61% (06)	99.6% (06)	99% (03)	99% (03)	77% (06)
Internet Users / As % of Population (2005)[27]	205.327M (05) / 69%	1,018M (05) / 16%	37.6M (05) / 63%	86.3M (05) / 68%	123M (06) / 9%	60M (05) / 5%	23.7M (05) / 17%	50.616M (06) / 61%	29.945M (06) / 49%	7.5M (05) / 11%
# Top 100 Universities in Each Country[28]	44		14	5	3	0	0	3	3	0
POPULATION										
Net Migration Rate (migrants per 1000 people)—2006[29]	3.18	Not Avail	2.18	0	-.39	-.07	1.03	2.18	0.66	-0.48
Immigrants with Bachelor Degree[30]	25.8% (00)	Not Avail	19% (app. 01)	Not Avail	Not Avail	Not Avail	Not Avail	Not Avail	Not Avail	Not Avail
Median Age (years) (2006)[31]	36.6	28	39.6	43.5	33.2	24.8	38.2	43	39	25.8
Population (2007)[32]	301.1M	6,602M	60.8M	127.4M	1,322M	1,129M	141.4M	82.4M	63.7M	65.4M
Life Expectancy at Birth (years)[33]	77 (04) / 75 (90)	67 (04) / 65 (90)	79 (04) / 76 (90)	82 (04) / 79 (90)	71 (04) / 69 (90)	63 (04) / 59 (90)	65 (04) / 69 (90)	78 (04) / 75 (90)	80 (04) / 77 (90)	71 (04) / 65 (90)
CULTURAL										
Movie Revenue ($) / Ticket Sales[34]	9.49B (06) / 2.6B tickets worldwide (06)	23.2B (05) / 7.45B tickets (05)	1.5B (05) / 165–170M tickets (05)	0.2026B Yen (06) / 164M tickets (06)	.737B revenue (06)	1.75B (06)—(movie industry revenue / 3B tickets worldwide (06)	340M (05) / 92M tickets (05)	121.3M tickets (05)	176M tickets (05)	Not Avail

Music Sales (# of albums in top 10 sales globally with artist from country) (2006/2005/2004)[35]	6 (06)/ 7 (05)/ 6 (04)	10	3 (06)/ 3 (05)/ 2 (04)	NA	NA	NA	NA	1 (06)	NA
Music Sales by Company (# of albums in top 10 produced by company with HQs in country) (2006/2005/2004)[35]	9 (06)/ 8 (05)/ 8 (04)	10	3 (06)-two dual/ 2 (05)/ 2 (04)	NA	NA	NA	NA	NA	NA
Exports of Recorded Media 2002 ($) (Records, Discs, and Tapes)[36]	3,070M	1,640M	371M	255M/ 255M (Hong Kong)	191M	59M	2,280M	741M	76M
Imports of Recorded Media 2002 ($) (Records, Discs, and Tapes)[37]	1,360M	1,950M	778M	873M/ 279M (Hong Kong)	708M	59M	1,490M	1,400M	7M
Exports of Audiovisual Media 2002 ($) (photo and cinema film and videogames)[36]	345M	330M	1.21B	2.3B/ 3.5M (Hong Kong)	16M	786,000	639M	94M	0
Imports of Audiovisual Media 2002 ($) (photo and cinema film and videogames)[37]	4,090M	711M	261M	58M/ 657M (Hong Kong)	5M	2.79M	889M	527M	0.314M

Measures of State Power (*continued*)

Measure	US	Rest of World	UK	Japan	China	India	Russia	Germany	France	Iran
Exports of Books 2002 ($) (printed books, brochures, and leaflets)[36]	1,920M		1,810M	108M	409M/258M (Hong Kong)	43M	240M	1,260M	519M	1M
Imports of Books 2002 ($) (printed books, brochures, and leaflets)[37]	2,090M		1,270M	330M	97M/473M (Hong Kong)	79M	103M	632M	541M	20M
Exports of Newspapers and Periodicals 2002 ($)[36]	880M		744M	34M	4.6M/35M (Hong Kong)	13M	15M	711M	369M	Not Reported
Imports of Newspapers and Periodicals 2002 ($)[37]	303M		301M	127M	52.7M/24.3M (Hong Kong)	5M	164M	329M	402M	.0529M
Exports of Heritage Goods 2002 ($) (Collections & Collectors' Pieces, Antiques of an age exceeding 100 years)[36]	143M		1,050M	8.1M	2.37M/490,000 (Hong Kong)	918,000	1.3M	74M	189M	Not Reported
Imports of Heritage Goods 2002 ($) (Collections & Collectors' Pieces, Antiques of an age exceeding 100 years)[37]	1,390M		673M	51M	729,000/89M (Hong Kong)	262,000	533,200	42M	67M	Not Reported
Most Influential Language (points/ranking)—1997[38]	37/1st (English)		same as U.S.	10/8th	13/6th	9/10th (Hindi/Urdu)	16/4th	12/7th	23/2nd	NA
# Who Speak Language as First Language—1997 Estimate[38]	>330M (worldwide)			<125M	>1,100M	>250M (Hindi/Urdu)	>160M	<100M	>75M	NA

# of Secondary Speakers—# / Ranking—1997[38]	150M / 2nd (worldwide)		8M/9th	20M/7th	NA	125M/3rd	9M/8th	190M/1st	NA
International Tourism Receipts ($) / % of World Share / % Change (05/04) —2005[39]	81.7B / 56.5% / 9.6%	680B / 7.5%	30.7B / 8.8% / 8.7%	29.3B / 21.1% / 13.8% (Hong Kong— 10.3B / 7.4% / 14.3%)	7.356B / 5.3% / 20.2%	5.466B / 1.6% / 4.6%	29.2B / 8.4% / 5.6%	42.3B / 12.1% / 3.5%	1.074B (2004) / NA / 4% (04/03)
Number of Tourists / % of World Share / % Change (05/04) —2005[39]	49.4M / 37% / 7.2%	806.3M	30M / 6.8% / 8%	46.8M / 30.1% / 12.1% (Hong Kong— 14.8M / 9.5% / 8.2%)	3.915M / 2.5% / 13.2%	19.94M / 4.5% / 0.2%	21.5M / 4.9% / 6.8%	76M / 17.2% / 1.2%	1.659M (2004) / NA / 7.3% (04/03)

a http://new.stjohns.edu/media/3/dfed5458faec4735b8369578d1264 5d9.pdf

b http://www.kauffman.org/pdf/eship_bankruptcy_061505.pdf

c Note: over two-thirds of the world's 785 million illiterate adults are found in only eight countries (India, China, Bangladesh, Pakistan, Nigeria, Ethiopia, Indonesia, and Egypt); of all the illiterate adults in the world, two-thirds are women; extremely low literacy rates are concentrated in three regions, South and West Asia, Sub-Saharan Africa, and the Arab states, where around one-third of the men and half of all women are illiterate (2005 est.).

Source Notes:

[ECONOMICS]

1 GDP (2005 actual): World Development Indicators database, World Bank, 23 April 2007.

2 GDP (purchasing power parity 2006): (Central Intelligence Agency, World Factbook, Rank Order—GDP, 5/8/2007).

3 GDP (proportion of global GDP): derived from World Development Indicators Database, World Bank, 23 April 2007.

4 GDP composition by sector: (Central Intelligence Agency, World Factbook, United States, www.cia.gov/cia/publications/factbook/print).

Measures of State Power (*Source Notes continued*)

5 Foreign direct investment net flows: World Bank (devdata.worldbank.org/data-query/SMResult.asp).

6 Foreign direct investment flows 2005: (United Nations Conference on Trade and Development, World Investment Report 2006).

7 Workers remittances received ($ 2005): World Bank (devdata.worldbank.org/data-query/SMResult.asp).

8 Remittances sent abroad ($ 2004): World Bank 2/25/2007 (econ.worldbank.org/external/default/main?pagePK=64165259&theSitePK=469372 . . .); *see also* Government Accountability Office, Report to the Committee on Banking, Housing, and Urban Affairs, US Senate, International Remittances: Different Estimation Methodologies Produce Different Results (March 2006), Congressional Budget Office, Remittances: International Payments by Migrants (May 2005), and Manuel Orozco, Worker Remittances in an International Scope (Inter-American Dialogue Research Series, March 2003).

9 Foreign holders of US treasuries ($ February 2007): (www.ustreas.gov/tic/mfh.txt, 4/19/2007).

10 Foreign exchange holdings of country currencies ($): International Monetary Fund Statistics Department COFER database, 2006).

11 Business bankruptcies/total bankruptcies (#>1): (http://new.stjohns.edu/media/3/dfed5458faec4735b8369578d1264d5d9.pdf; http://www.kauffman.org/pdf/eship_bankruptcy_061505.pdf).

12 Time required to start a business: World Bank (devdata.worldbank.org/data-query/SMResult.asp, 5/8/2007).

13 Fortune global 500 companies (#); (*Fortune,* July 24, 2006).

14 # Foreign companies listed on stock market (March 2007); World Federation of Exchanges, *Focus,* (April 2007—N 170, p. 37).

15 Bank branches per 100,000 people (2001–2004): World Bank, *World Development Indicators 2006,* Table 5.5: Financial access, stability, and efficiency.

16 Charitable giving (as a % of GDP, 2004): Sally Clegg and Cathy Pharoah, CAF Briefing Paper: International Comparisons of Charitable Giving (November 2006).

17 Highest federal marginal tax rate (2004): World Bank, World Development Indicators 2006, Table 5.6: Tax Policies.

[MILITARY]

18 Defense spending, and defense spending as a % of GDP: (International Institute for Strategic Studies, *The Military Balance 2007,* pp. 406–411).

[INTELLECTUAL]

19 Patent applications (resident/non-resident/total): World Intellectual Property Organization, WIPO Patent Report: Statistics on Worldwide Patent Activities 2006.

20 Nobel prizes (%)/ # received: JINFO, United States Nobel Prize Winners (www.jinfo.org/US_Nobel_Prizes.html).

21 % of foreign students (2004): UNESCO Institute for Statistics, Global Education Digest 2006, Figure 19: distribution of the world's total mobile students, p. 47.

22 Foreign students in given country (2004): Table 9, Internationally Mobile Students in Tertiary Education by Host Country, pp. 130–131; see also American Council on Education, Center for International Initiatives Issue Brief: "Students on the Move: The Future of International Students in the United States," Table 5: International Student Enrollment, pp. 10–11.

23 Students studying abroad (2004): Institute for Statistics, Global Education Digest 2006, Table 10: International Flows of Mobile Students, pp. 132–135.

24 R&D expenditures ($ PPP): Organization for Economic Cooperation and Development, Main Science and Technology Indicators (2004, see appendix table 4-42; *see also* National Science Foundation, Science and Engineering Indicators 2006, Figure 4-27, 4-45, 4-33 (www.nsf.gov/statistics/seind06/c4/fog04-27.htm).

25 Expenditures for R&D (% of GDP, 1996–2004): World Bank, World Development Indicators 2006, Table 5.11. From same source: researchers in R&D (per million people, 1996–2004); scientific and technical journal articles; royalty and license fees (receipts, $ millions, 2004); trademark applications filed (resident/non-resident, 2002).

26 Education (literacy age 15+/% with Bachelor's degree): United Nations Institute for Statistics, Literacy and Non-Formal Education System (September 2006); *see also* Central Intelligence Agency, The World Factbook (www.cia.gov/cia/publications/factbook/print/us.html).

27 Internet users/as % of population (2007 population statistics): Central Intelligence Agency, The World Factbook (www.cia.gov/cia/publications/factbook/print/us.html); *see also* Population Reference Bureau, 2005 World Population Data Sheet.

28 # top 100 universities; *Newsweek International*, "Top 100 Global Universities" (www.msnbc.msn.com/id/14321230/site/newsweek/print/1/displaymode/1098/).

[POPULATION]

29 Net migrants (per 1000 people): Central Intelligence Agency, The World Factbook (www.cia.gov/cia/publications/factbook/print).

30 Immigrants with Bachelor's degree: U.S. Census Bureau, Profile of the Foreign-Born Population in the United States: 2000 (December 2001, p. 36); UK Home Office, Migrants in the UK: Their Characteristics and Labour Market Outcomes and Impacts (RDS Occasional Paper 82, December 2002, pg. 12–14).

31 Median age (years): Central Intelligence Agency, The World Factbook (www.cia.gov/cia/publications/factbook/print).

32 Population (2007): Central Intelligence Agency, The World Factbook (www.cia.gov/cia/publications/factbook/print).

33 Life expectancy at birth: World Bank, World Development Indicators 2006.

[CULTURAL]

34 Movie revenue ($)/ticket sales: Motion Picture Association Worldwide Market Research and Analysis, 2006 International Theatrical Market (April 2007); Motion Picture Producers Association of Japan, Statistics of Film Industry in Japan Year 2000–2006 (www.eiren.org/statistics_c/index.html); Paula M. Miller, "Special Report: Entertainment," *China Business Review*, (www.chinabusinessreview.com/public/0703/miller.html); Krittivas Mukherjee, Bollywood toys with Hollywood-style spinoffs, (1/30/2007); "European Ticket Sales Took Hit in '05," *Hollywood Reporter* (January 10, 2006).

35 Music sales (# of albums in top 10 sales globally (06/05/04): IFPI, Top 50 Albums of 2004, 2005, 2006. Music by company: IFPI National Groups/Chart Companies.

36 Exports of recorded media (records, CD, tapes 2002): UNESCO Institute for Statistics, International Flows of Selected Cultural Goods and Services, 1994–2003. From same source: Exports of audiovisual media ($ photo, cinema, video games 2002); exports of books ($, printed books, brochures, leaflets, 2002); exports of newspapers and periodicals ($ 2002); exports of heritage goods ($ 2002, collections and collectors' pieces, antiques exceeding 100 years).

37 Imports of recorded media (2002) UNESCO Institute for Statistics, International Flows of Selected Cultural Goods and Services, 1994–2003. Also: Imports of audiovisual media (2002); imports of books ($, 2002); imports of newspapers, periodicals ($, 2002) imports of heritage goods ($, 2002).

38 Most influential language (points/ranking); George Weber, *Top Languages* (www.andaman.org/BOOK/reprints/weber/rep-weber.htm, pp. 1–17). Also: # who speak as 1st language; # of secondary speakers.

39 International tourism receipts ($/% of world share/% change 05–04): World Tourism Organization, Tourism Highlights, 2006 Edition (www.unwto.org). Also: Number of tourists/% of world share/% change 05–04.

About the Author

★ ★ ★

KORI N. SCHAKE is a research fellow at the Hoover Institution and holds the Distinguished Chair in International Security Studies at the U.S. Military Academy at West Point. During the 2008 presidential campaign, she was Senior Policy Advisor to John McCain.

Previously, she has served in senior policy positions, including deputy director of policy planning at the State Department, director of defense strategy and requirements on the National Security Council, and posts in the Office of the Secretary of Defense and the office of the Joint Chiefs of Staff chairman.

She has been a member of the faculties of the Johns Hopkins School of Advanced International Studies, the University of Maryland School of Public Affairs, and the National Defense University.

She holds a PhD and two MAs from the University of Maryland and a BA from Stanford University. Her previous writing includes *Transatlantic Relations after the Elections: The Coming Crisis of High Expectations; The Strategic Implications of a Nuclear Armed Iran* (with Judith Yaphe); and *The Berlin Crises, 1958–1961* (with John Gearson).

Index

★ ★ ★